# CALIFORNIA

# CALIFORNIA BY ROAD

# CELEBRATE THE STATES
# CALIFORNIA

## Linda Jacobs Altman

# BENCHMARK BOOKS

## MARSHALL CAVENDISH
## NEW YORK

Benchmark Books
Marshall Cavendish Corporation
99 White Plains Road
Tarrytown, New York 10591-9001

Library of Congress Cataloging-in-Publication Data
Altman, Linda Jacobs, date
California / by Linda Jacobs Altman.
p.   cm. — (Celebrate the states)
Includes index.
Summary: An overview of the geography, history, economy, and people of California.
ISBN 0-7614-0111-3 (lib. bdg.)
1. California—Juvenile literature. [1. California.] I. Title. II. Series.
F861.3.A45  1997   979.4—dc20      96-11537      CIP   AC

Maps and graphics supplied by Oxford Cartographers, Oxford, England

Photo research by Ellen Barrett Dudley

Cover photo: *Image Bank*, Romilly Lockyer

The photographs in this book are used by permission and through the courtesy of: *Image Bank*: David W. Hamilton, 6-7, 18; Place, 13; G. V. Faint, 15, 113; Stuart Dee, 26; Marc Romanelli, 28; Brett H. Froomer, 66; Andrea Pistolesi, 94; Jeff Hunter, 105, 111; G. K. and Vikki Hart, 115; Michael Melford, 127; Morton Beebe, 128; Ulf E. Wallin, 138; Don Landwehrl, back cover. *Photo Researchers, Inc.*: Andy Levin, 10-11; Louisa Preston, 22; Francois Gohier, 23 (top); Tom McHugh, 25; Jim Corwin, 46-47; ChromoSohm/Joseph Sohm, 56, 71, 102-103; David R. Frazier, 63, 106; Bill Aron, 65; Spencer Grant, 68-69, 88-89; Lawrence Migdale, 75, 81; Susan McCartney, 76; Gordon E. Smith, 84; George Ranalli, 108; William Townsend, 112; Calvin Larson, 121. *Animals Animals*: Breck P. Kent, 23 (bottom). *Collection of the Oakland Museum of California, The Oakland Museum Kahn Collection*: 30-31. *Widener Library*: 33. *Seaver Center for Western History Research, Natural History Research, Natural History Museum of Los Angeles County*: 35. *Crocker Art Museum, Sacramento, CA: E. B. Crocker Collection*: 36. *Corbis-Bettmann*: 38, 135. *Dorothea Lang Collection, The Oakland Museum of California, The City of Oakland. Gift of Paul S. Tayler*: 43, 45. *UPI/Corbis-Bettmann*: 50, 57, 74, 93, 130, 132 (bottom). *Reuters/Corbis-Bettmann*: 51, 83, 91, 99, 101. *Reuters/Lou Dematteis/Archive Photos*: 52. © Nita Winters: 60, 86. *California Department of Parks and Recreation, Photographic Archives*: 79. *Photofest*: 96, 97, 131, 132 (top), 133, 136 (left and right). © Noella Ballenger: 116, 137. *Peter Arnold*: 124.

Printed in Italy

1   3   5   6   4   2

# CONTENTS

# CALIFORNIA IS . . .

## California is a place . . .

. . . where "the mind is troubled by some . . . suspicion that things had better work here, because here, beneath that immense bleached sky, is where we run out of continent."

—American novelist Joan Didion

" . . . where people come to make their fortunes . . . where beautiful women are 'discovered' in drug stores, and a man can turn a mouse into an empire." —writer M.G. Lord in *Forever Barbie*

## . . . and it is people.

"I guess it's . . . snobbery. . . . It has something to do with just spending money. . . . The way I look at it, I can buy myself anything I can afford. We're just fast livers out here in California."

—business executive Elliot Sopkin,
on buying an expensive custom stereo for his car

"Californians are a race of people; they are not merely inhabitants of a state." —American writer O. Henry

## California is dearly loved . . .

"Cross a time zone or two. Say the word, California. Watch the reactions. The sweet look of memories and wishes crosses [people's] faces. . . . they'll tell you about relatives who moved West. About tawny sunsets over the ocean. About the glitter . . . of the big cities and the rugged quiet of the mountains. About stars, and money won and lost, and dreams left far behind."

—newspaper columnist Anita Creamer

## . . . and passionately disliked.

"The people are unreal. The flowers are unreal, they don't smell. The fruit is unreal, it doesn't taste of anything. The whole place is a glaring, gaudy, nightmarish set, built upon the desert."

—actress Ethel Barrymore

"We could build a high fence around California and post psychiatrists at the border gates. Nobody would be permitted to leave it without passing a sanity test. . . . For years California's major export to the rest of the country has not been its fruits and vegetables; it has been craziness. It comes in many forms—bad TV shows, bad architecture, junk foods, auto worship and creepy life-styles. . . . You name it: If it babbles and its eyeballs are blazed, it probably comes from California." —newspaper columnist Mike Royko

---

*Anything* can and does happen in California; that's part of its charm. It is a mass of contradictions. It is sunstruck beaches, snow-capped mountains, and pastel deserts; great, sprawling cities and little country towns. It is movie stars and theme parks and hot tubs. Most of all, it is people; millions of ordinary folk, from different walks of life and different cultures. Together, they are creating a society that is as rich and varied as the California landscape.

# 1 THE LAY OF THE LAND

**O**n the map, California looks something like a boomerang; long and narrow, with a noticeable bend about one-third of the way down. It has the highest and lowest places in the contiguous United States: Mount Whitney at 14,494 feet above sea level and Death Valley, at 282 feet below.

Once, the northern mountains were active volcanoes and the low deserts of the south were covered by a primeval sea. Glaciers carved deep river canyons into the western face of the Sierra Nevada. The San Andreas Fault slipped and slid and folded onto itself, endlessly changing the shape of the coastal lands into what we call California today.

## THE LAND FORMS

California measures 780 miles through its center and contains ten distinct natural regions—more than any other state. Six of these regions are mountainous, three are deserts, and one is a great, fertile valley in the center of the state.

**Mountains.** In the northwest corner of the state, the heavily forested Klamath Mountains reach eight-thousand-foot elevations. This range includes the soaring Trinity Alps, which were carved by ancient glaciers. To the east lies the volcanic Cascade Range. Its

*Bristlecone pines in the Patriarch Grove of the White Mountains in eastern California. Bristlecones live longer than any other tree because they grow slowly and live in cool, dry areas that have few harmful insects and diseases.*

tallest peak, Mount Shasta, is the cone of a long dormant volcano. Mount Lassen, some eighty-five miles to the southeast, is one of only two volcanoes that have erupted in the twentieth century in the continental United States. Mount Lassen last erupted in 1921.

The Coast Ranges follow the Pacific shoreline from the Klamath Mountains down to Point Concepción. They average two thousand to four thousand feet in elevation. The northern sections are covered with trees and dotted with fertile valleys. In the south, forest gives way to chaparral; a dense, mixed brush that grows in semiarid conditions.

The San Andreas Fault, a fracture in the earth's crust, cuts through the Coast Ranges. This makes the area prone to earthquakes. There are hundreds of these faults throughout California; the San Andreas is simply the largest and best known. It is about six hundred miles long, and up to a mile wide.

In the eastern part of the state lies the towering Sierra Nevada range. It is a formidable barrier, fifty to eighty miles wide and stretching for about four hundred miles from north to south. Along the western slopes are deep river canyons such as Yosemite Valley. The foothills are rich in mineral deposits, including gold; it was here that the gold rush of 1849 began.

Farther south are the Transverse and Peninsular Ranges. The Transverse Ranges, also called the Los Angeles Ranges, define the southern California landscape; all land routes from the north and east pass through them. Major passes include Gaviota, Cajon, Tejon, and San Gorgonio. The Peninsular Ranges, also called the San Diego Range, rise in the southwest and extend south into Baja (lower) California, which is part of Mexico.

**The Central Valley.** This oval valley, which runs down the center of California, is one of the most fertile agricultural areas in the world. The rich valley soil is washed down from the surrounding mountains, making it excellent for many crops: cotton, grains, nuts, rice, fruits, sugar beets, and all kinds of vegetables.

The valley is a workaday place. Sophisticates from the coastal cities have looked down on it for years. After Ronald Reagan was elected governor of California, his wife, Nancy, had only one thing to say about living in Sacramento: "Thank heavens we can escape to Beverly Hills on the weekends."

**The Deserts.** Part of the huge area known as the Great Basin lies along the Nevada border. As it reaches into northern California, the basin turns into a treeless highland dotted with lava beds. The southeastern portion includes Death Valley, which extends 140 miles through eastern California and western Nevada.

To the south and east of this basin are the Colorado and Mojave

*The skull of a bighorn sheep in the sand dunes of Death Valley.*

# LAND AND WATER

Yreka

Weed • Alturas • *Goose Lake*

Arcata

Eureka

*Shasta Lake*

Redding • *Lassen Volcanic NP* • Susanville

Red Bluff

*Cape Mendocino*

Chico • Paradise

Ukiah

Williams • Yuba City

*Clear L.*

Santa Rosa • Woodland

*Lake Berryessa* • ◉ Sacramento

*Lake Tahoe*

*Pt. Reyes*

Berkeley • Stockton

San Francisco • Oakland

San Jose • Modesto • Turlock • *Mono Lake*

*San Joaquin R.* • Merced

*Monterey Bay* • Salinas

Monterey • Fresno

▲ Mount Whitney *(14,494 ft)* • *Death Valley*

Visalia

Tulare • Porterville

Paso Robles • *Tulare Lake*

San Luis Obispo • *Buena Vista Lake Bed* • Bakersfield • Ridgecrest

Santa Maria • Mojave • *Mojave Desert* • Baker

Lompoc • Barstow

*Pt. Conception* • Santa Barbara • Lancaster • Ludlow

*Santa Barbara Channel* • *Mojave Desert*

Oxnard • Pasadena • San Bernardino

*Santa Rosa I.* • *Santa Cruz I.* • Los Angeles • Riverside

Santa Ana

Long Beach • Indio

*Santa Catalina I.* • Temecula • Palm Springs • Blythe

Oceanside • Escondido • *Salton Sea (235ft Below Sea Level)*

*San Clemente I.* • *Gulf of Santa Catalina*

San Diego • El Centro • Yuma

Calexico

Deserts. The Mojave is largely barren, with great pastel vistas that seem to stretch on forever. "This place can seem grim by daylight," said one long-time resident. "Come sunset, though . . . nothing's prettier in all the world." The Colorado is made up of the Coachella and Imperial Valleys, areas that have been irrigated to provide excellent farmland.

## THE CLIMATE

With such wide variety of land forms, it is not surprising that California also has many different climates. The highest temperature ever recorded in the state is 134 degrees; the lowest, minus 45. There are five kinds of climate in California, called coastal, valley, foothill, mountain, and desert.

On the southern California coast, the beaches are sunny and the winters mild. In the north, the weather tends to be colder. San Francisco is famous for its ocean breezes and the fog that rolls in from the sea. Even in summer, mornings and evenings are "sweater weather." As Mark Twain once put it: "The coldest winter I ever spent was a summer I spent in San Francisco."

The climate of the Sacramento and San Joaquin Valleys is hot and dry in the summer, cold and humid in the winter. Valley winters are noted for the ground-hugging tule fog that occurs in marshy areas. (Tule is an Aztec name for marsh vegetation.) This fog does not come in from the ocean, like the fog in San Francisco; tule fog seems to rise from the ground, turning everything a soft, silvery gray. "You don't drive through this stuff," said a long-haul truck driver. "You sit 'till it decides to be over."

*Fog blankets the Golden Gate Bridge in San Francisco.*

In the foothills, temperatures are similar to those in the valleys but there are no tule fogs. The foothill areas rarely get snow.

In the mountains summers are warm and winters rainy, with heavy snow at the higher elevations. The Sierra Nevada, for example, gets an average of 445 inches of snow each year. Californians watch each season's snowpack with avid interest; it is an important source of water. When it melts in the spring, it flows into the rivers and streams that carry water to the lowlands.

In the desert, the atmosphere has so little humidity that even one hundred-plus days are bearable. As desert dwellers are fond of saying, it's a dry heat, meaning that it's less punishing than the heat that comes with high humidity. Desert nights are usually cool and pleasant, even in summer. Winter nights can plunge to subzero temperatures.

## THE WATERWAYS

California's principal rivers are the Sacramento in the north and the San Joaquin in the south. Most of the other large rivers in the state flow into one of these two. In the south, the Colorado River flows down from the Rocky Mountains to form California's southeastern border.

California has relatively few natural lakes. The largest body of freshwater entirely within the state is Clear Lake, some one hundred miles north of San Francisco. Lake Tahoe, which is larger, is located partly in Nevada. Other natural lakes are Goose, Eagle, and Mono, all in the northern part of the state.

The Salton Sea, in the desert of the Imperial Valley, was once the bed of an ancient lake. In 1905, the Colorado River flooded, filling the basin and creating an inland sea that lies some 232 feet below sea level. Because the Salton Sea has no natural outlets, water that flows into it is trapped there. Over the years, that water has become almost as salty as the ocean itself.

Most of California's freshwater lakes are actually reservoirs. Water has always been a problem in California: the northern part of

## CELEBRATING SWALLOWS

Every year on March 19, thousands of people gather in southern California to witness a small miracle: the return of the swallows to San Juan Capistrano. Legend says they all arrive on that one day. Science says there's nothing special about the nineteenth, since swallows arrive throughout the month of March.

Californians ignore the experts. For more than sixty years, a joyous festival has marked the day of the swallows' return. The town patriarch rings the mission bells to welcome the migrants home. Mariachi stroll through the crowd, trumpets, guitars, and voices combining in exuberant Mexican songs. Brightly costumed folk dancers perform in the square.

Every now and then, a single voice will rise over the noise of the crowd: "I see one!" Everybody looks up. The sighting may be a pigeon or a seagull; then again, it could be the first swallow of the season. Amid the music and laughter and general commotion, the festival continues. Sooner or later, someone will spot that first swallow. In the meantime, there's plenty to do and to see at this annual tribute to a genuine California legend.

the state has it, the southern part does not. Southern California gets only 30 percent of the state's annual rainfall but uses 80 percent of the water supply. Lakes Shasta, Berryessa, Folsom, Isabella, Cachuma, and Arrowhead are just a few of the better-known reservoirs. From these artificial lakes, a vast system of aqueducts moves the water to where it is needed.

## GROWING THINGS

California's plant and animal life is as varied as the land it occupies. In the coastal woodlands of the north, giant redwoods stand as tall as 370 feet and live for more than two thousand years. Another redwood species, the famed giant sequoia of the Sierra Nevada, has an even longer lifespan: 3,200 years. The bristlecone pine of the east-central mountains is oldest of all. One tree in the Inyo National Forest is 4,600 years old.

Oak, aspen, eucalyptus, and palm are closely associated with California. Black oak and aspen grow in the mountains, while eucalyptus and canyon live oak are found throughout the state. Scrub oak and palm appear in the south.

Other California vegetation includes myrtle and flowering dogwood in the mountains, and the golden poppy (the state flower), which once spread over the foothills and valleys of the state. The Mojave Desert is home to many kinds of drought-resistant succulents (fleshy plants that store water in their tissues).

Each of California's environments has its resident wildlife. The desert is home to bighorn sheep, wild burros, coyotes, hares, and many kinds of lizards. Chaparral areas have rabbits, rattlesnakes,

California poppies turn the landscape into a blaze of orange.

A rare feral (wild) donkey in the Mojave Desert, a vast wasteland covering twenty-five thousand square miles.

A giant sequoia tree in Yosemite National Park (left). Sequoia were named after the Cherokee, Sequoia, who invented a written alphabet and system of writing to preserve the culture of his people.

rodents, and deer, while the mountains have cougars and bears.

Rivers and lakes contain salmon, bass, and trout, while coastal waters have shellfish, perch, and tuna. Marine mammals such as seals, sea lions, otters, and dolphins make their home off the California coast.

An amazing variety of birds live in the state or make it a stop on their migratory rounds. Seagulls, pelicans, and terns live along the coast; spotted owls in the forests of the north; rare California condors in the Transverse Ranges of the south. Quail flourish in all areas of the state.

In the central valley town of Colusa, anyone who finds an abandoned nest takes the eggs to farmer Roger Moore. For thirty years, Moore has run a volunteer hatchery for ducks, pheasants, marsh hawks, valley quail—any kind of bird that happens his way. He cares for the hatchlings until they can survive on their own. In 1993 friends came from all around to help celebrate the release of the ten thousandth baby duck raised from rescued eggs. "It just takes a little work," Moore said, "or make that a lot of work by a lot of people, but it's worth it."

## THE PEOPLE

California is the most populous state in the nation, with 31,589,153 people as of July 1995. More than 91 percent of these people live in the densely populated urban areas along the coast. The five counties of southern California have more people than the other fifty-three counties combined.

The difference is quite dramatic. For example, Del Norte County,

# SAVING THE CALIFORNIA CONDOR

When rancher Eben McMillan first settled in San Luis Obispo county, he got used to the big shadows that crossed his lawn every day at lunchtime. He would look up and see a majestic black condor outlined against the sky. Condors are the largest land bird in North America, with an average weight of twenty pounds and a wing span of nine to ten feet. There were hundreds of them back in the 1940s when Eben bought his land. By 1982, only twenty-three remained.

Environmentalists began a habitat-restoration and captive-breeding program. Ten years later, the total condor population was up to sixty-three, with fifty-six of them still living in captivity. A massive program to return condors to the wild had its ups and downs. Captive-bred birds had no fear of humans and no knowledge of hazards like power lines.

Animal behavior experts went to work. They taught condors not to land on power poles by setting up fake poles that gave mild shocks. Professional trainers deliberately harassed the birds so they would learn to avoid humans. With programs such as these, the Condor Recovery Team hopes that the birds will soon begin breeding in the wild and rearing their own young.

*Los Angeles at sunset. The city is the major business, financial, and trade center of the western United States. When a captain in the Spanish army and a Franciscan explored the region in 1769, they named it* Nuestra Señora la Reina de Los Angeles de Porciúncula, *"Our Lady the Queen of the Angels of Porciúncula," after a chapel in Italy.*

which borders Oregon in the northwest, has a population of only 23,460; San Diego County, which borders Mexico in the southwest, has 2,498,016. The San Francisco Bay area, which is the major metropolitan center of the north, has fewer than two million people. The Los Angeles area has nearly nine million.

Geography and weather account for much of this population pattern. The northernmost part of the state is mountainous, with thin soil and difficult terrain. Its coastline is rugged and rocky; its weather, cold and rainy. The south has flatland for building and farming, white sand beaches that stretch from Santa Barbara to San Diego, and a mild climate that permits year-round agriculture. People just naturally settled there.

Farther inland, the southern deserts were sparsely populated until improved irrigation and water-transport systems made it possible for people to live and work there. In the eighties and nineties, thousands left the metropolitan Los Angeles area for cleaner air and lower housing costs. Many of them continued to commute to their jobs, driving great distances on crowded freeways. "The only way we could afford a decent house was to move out here to the boondocks," said a mechanic who lives fifty miles from his workplace.

## THE ENVIRONMENT

Ever since California became a state, it has experienced rapid population growth, as much as 50 percent in some years. During the 1980s, for example, California's overall population grew at a rate of more than 25 percent. This rapid growth has taken its toll on the environment. For decades, residents of Los Angeles have coped with the brownish haze that hangs in the air on windless days. Back in 1905, somebody dubbed it "smog" (from SMoke and fOG). At the time, smog was something of a joke. It was bad, yes; but most people didn't realize how bad.

*High-speed freeways ring downtown Los Angeles. People depend heavily on their cars to travel around the sprawling city, but the cars cause such air pollution that the city is often covered by smog.*

By the nineties, nobody was laughing. Smog has become a problem all over the state. Efforts to clean up the air center on controlling automobile emissions. This is no easy task, because Californians love their cars. Long commutes in bumper-to-bumper traffic have become part of the lifestyle. Responses to pollution include smog control devices on cars and trucks, unleaded gasoline, and development of public transit systems.

Water, land, and wildlife also need care. Strict laws protect the environment from contamination. Recycling has become a way of life, reducing the demand on landfills. Californians are learning to protect their natural resources for themselves and for future generations.

# 2 CALIFORNIA YESTERDAYS

"*Kings River Canyon,*" *by William Keith*

**S**panish explorers first entered California in 1542. Missionaries followed, building a chain of twenty-one churches along what became known as El Camino Real, or "the Royal Road." California was part of Mexico until the Treaty of Guadalupe Hidalgo ceded it to the United States in 1848.

That same year, gold was discovered at John Sutter's mill, in the Sierra foothills. Fortune hunters swarmed over the area, chasing their dreams and adding their deeds to California's rich history.

## NATIVE INHABITANTS

The native peoples of California lived in small tribal bands; they built no cities, crowned no kings, and made no formal laws. They lived off the land, gathering nuts, seeds, roots, and berries to eat. Mountain tribes hunted deer and small game. Coastal tribes harvested fish and shellfish from the sea.

Though the tribes were not unified into a nation, they did have a great deal in common. They lived in comfortable huts or tepees, made of local materials: redwood bark in the north, brush in the chaparral country, tule (swampgrass) in the wetlands of the river deltas.

They had rich cultural traditions. People sang songs while they went about their daily tasks, and told stories around an evening campfire. The Pomos of northern California were skilled basket makers. They could weave straw so tightly that it would hold water. The Chumash of southern California made elaborate cave paintings that were probably connected with some of their religious rituals. Other tribes had other specialties.

## EXPLORERS AND MISSIONARIES

The area that is now California was discovered in 1542 by João Rodrígues Cabrilho. He was a Portuguese-born sailor who served under Hernán Cortés. Cabrilho sailed north from Mexico to find a

*This is one of the earliest pictures of native Californians. These fishermen appeared in George Shelrock's book* Voyage Around the World, *published in 1726.*

Northwest Passage that would connect the Atlantic and Pacific oceans. Instead, he found California.

He thought he'd found a dream. A popular adventure story of the day told of a fabulous island in the western sea. It was inhabited by Amazon warriors and ruled by a queen named Calafia. The explorers may have named the new land in her honor.

California was a wondrous place. It had abundant resources and no armies to protect them. The conquistadores (conquerors) set out to possess it. Missionaries followed, determined to convert native tribes to Christianity. The famous California missions came out of that period. There were twenty-one of them, from San Diego in the south (founded 1769) to Sonoma in the north (founded 1823).

## THE CALIFORNIOS

After the missionaries came the Californios: aristocrats who held vast territories under Spanish land grants. They led a gracious and privileged life. Like European nobility, the Californios cultivated swordsmanship, horsemanship, and the social graces. Work was for servants and other underlings.

Life was very different for poor people. They had little choice but to work for the patrón, or boss, who had almost total control of their lives. In southern California, three powerful families held most of the usable land: the Carrillos, with 320,000 acres; the de la Guerras, with 326,000; and the Picos, with 532,000. Northern California was divided among the Alvarados, Castros, Peraltas, and Vallejos.

The fortunes of the Californios changed after the Mexican-American War of 1846–1848. Mexico lost the war and on February 2, 1848, ceded California to the United States. The timing could not have been better for the Americans, or worse for the Spanish grandees. Just a week before the treaty was signed, a man named James Marshall discovered gold at Sutter's Mill.

*The extended Lugo family—proud Californios—pose for a group portrait in the mid-1800s*

Sunday Morning in the Mines *by Charles Nahl paints a romantic picture of life in a mining camp.*

## GOLD FEVER

With California an American possession, fortune hunters from the East and Midwest flooded into gold country. Instant towns sprang into being—rough settlements with names like Greenhorn Bar, Humbug Hill, and Whiskey Flat. They were lawless places, where life was cheap and everything else was expensive. Merchants sold food, clothing, and mining supplies for whatever the traffic would bear. Women could make small fortunes just taking in laundry or preparing home-cooked meals.

People came by land and by sea. They crossed the Sierras on foot, on horseback, or in covered wagons. They sailed around Cape

Horn and up the coast. In a few months, San Francisco grew from a sleepy village to a metropolitan port. There, fortune hunters docked on their way to gold country.

They all dreamed of great riches. Many returned with their dreams in shambles. Others did not return at all. For every story of fame and fortune, there were ten of heartbreak and death. People died of exposure, disease, and accident. Some were mauled by the fierce grizzly bears that roamed the foothills. Some took their own lives after failing to strike gold. Many fell victim to foul play, as gold fever turned would-be millionaires into claim jumpers and killers.

## A GOLD RUSH LAUNDRY

In 1849, pioneer doctor Felix Wierzbicki wrote of his experiences in gold country in *The Californians*. He devoted a great deal of attention to the subject of laundry. It was a real problem for the forty-niners, because washing clothes was "woman's work" and there were few women in the gold towns:

*The greatest privation that a bachelor [faces] is not being able to furnish himself with clean linen when he desires, as domestic service is so difficult to be kept up here for want of working women. To induce some of the few women that are here . . . to wash their linen for them, they have to court them besides paying six dollars a dozen.*

According to Wierzbicki, one forty-niner "paid" for his laundry with a marriage proposal, "because she refused to wash his clothes for him [otherwise]."

*Prospector George W. Northup from Minnesota poses with the tools of a goldminer and a sack of gold. The people swept up in the frenzy became known as the "forty-niners," after the year the gold rush began.*

"Since my arrival here," wrote forty-niner William Perkins, "three Mexicans and one [American] have been killed in street fights." Another forty-niner recorded the anonymous funerals of so many gold seekers: "It is an everyday occurence to see a coffin carried on the shoulders of two men, who are the only mourners and only witnesses of the burial of some stranger they do not know."

For good or ill, the gold rush shaped California society. The hardy dreamers who came west were not the sort to live by ordinary rules. They liked excitement and they liked taking chances. Schemes and dreams became a way of life. By the time California became a state in 1850, it was already El Dorado (the gilded), a place where the pursuit of happiness was everybody's favorite right.

## THE BIG FOUR

Even after the gold rush, California remained the fastest-growing state in the nation. By the turn of the century, it had a population of close to 1,500,000, up from almost 100,000 in 1850. The transcontinental railroad was completed in 1869, making the westward journey faster and less dangerous.

The "Big Four" who built the western railroad were Charles Crocker, Mark Hopkins, Collis P. Huntington, and Leland Stanford. They began as Sacramento businessmen, prosperous but far from rich. Huntington and Hopkins operated a hardware and mining-supply store; Crocker was a dry-goods merchant; Stanford, a lawyer. None of them knew anything about railroading. What they did know was how to promote an idea.

The transcontinental railroad was just the kind of visionary scheme they liked. They started with $6,000 and a half-formed idea, using methods that would land them in jail by today's standards. The Central Pacific Railroad issued $8,500,000 of stock on the strength of that $6,000.

Collis Huntington convinced Congress to give the railroad $25 million worth of government bonds and 4.5 million acres of public land. When time came to hire a contractor to do the actual building, the Big Four set up their own construction company and hired themselves. Charles Crocker headed the construction company, and he took the work very seriously: "Why, I used to go up and down that road in my car like a mad bull," he once said, "stopping along wherever there was anything amiss, and raising Old Nick with the boys that were not up to time."

# BANKS OF THE SACRAMENTO

This sea shanty was sung by sailors who took the *Flying Cloud,* the fastest clipper ship in the Black Ball line, on the dangerous route around Cape Horn to the California gold fields.

**Music by Stephen Foster ("Camptown Races")**

O we were the boys to make her go . . .
Around Cape Horn in the frost and snow . . . *Chorus*

Around Cape Stiff in seventy days . . .
Around Cape Stiff is a mighty long ways . . . *Chorus*

When we was tacking 'round Cape Horn . . .
I often wished I'd a never been born . . . *Chorus*

O the mate he whacked me around and around . . .
And I wished I was home all    safe and sound . . . *Chorus*

O when we got to the Frisco    docks . . .
The girls all were in their Sunday frocks . . . *Chorus*

Their crews laid 1,171 miles of track, starting from Sacramento and going over the Sierras to Promontory, Utah. There, the eastern and western lines joined. By that time, construction costs were over budget, the Big Four were millionaires, and the railroad was in debt up to its smokestacks. In spite of all that, the transcontinental brought new jobs, new markets—and new people—into California. Some came to make their fortunes, others came to find a home.

## HOORAY FOR HOLLYWOOD

In the early years of the twentieth century, moviemakers found both a fortune and a home in California. In the process, they transformed a sleepy little town called Hollywood into the glamour capitol of the world.

The motion picture industry actually began in New York, but outdoor filming was impossible during the winter months. What the movie pioneers needed was a land of endless summer and stunning landscapes. Southern California fit the bill.

Director D. W. Griffith is generally credited with transforming motion pictures from a passing fad into a thriving industry. Other filmmakers just placed the camera in front of a staging area and let it run. Griffith used it the way an artist uses brushes and paints: as a tool for shaping his ideas. He put the camera on a rolling platform so he could move it around; he created perspective with long, medium, and close-up shots; changed scenes with fade-ins and fade-outs; set a mood with angle shots and soft focus.

He also "invented" the movie star. In the earliest films, actors received neither screen credit nor pay for their work. Griffith put their names on the screen and transformed them into living legends. People lined up to see the latest Mary Pickford or Charlie Chaplin movie and scoured magazines and newspapers for gossip about the private lives of the stars. This kind of fame took its toll. Hollywood was not an easy or forgiving place: "To survive there," said actress Billie Burke, "you need the ambition of a Latin American revolutionary, the ego of a grand opera tenor, and the physical stamina of a cow pony."

By the 1920s, Hollywood was a magical name. Like the mother lode of the forty-niners, it became part of the California dream. After the stock market crash of 1929, thousands of desperate Americans looked to that dream to boost their sagging fortunes.

*A 1938 Dorothea Lange photograph captures a family from Oklahoma on the road in search of the California dream of a better life.*

## A GARDEN OF EDEN

The depression-era immigrants weren't looking for gold or hoping to become movie stars; they were just trying to survive. Nearly a million displaced sharecroppers came from the prairie states during the Great Depression. They had lost their money when the economy collapsed and their land when dust storms swirled through the area, killing crops and stripping topsoil.

They came west in broken-down jalopies, with all their possessions piled into the trunk, strapped on top, shoved into

## POPULATION GROWTH: 1850–1990

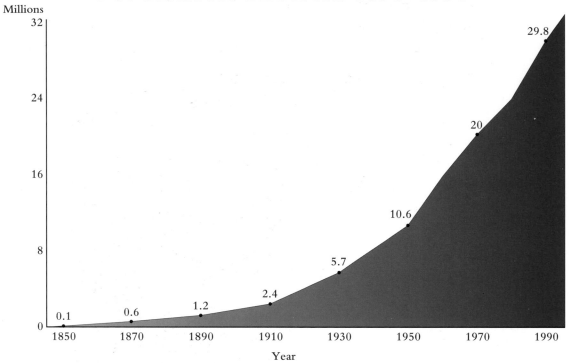

Millions

every nook and cranny of the car. They had heard that California had plenty of work and so much food it was free for the picking in fields and orchards all over the state. They soon learned the truth: ten or twenty people waited for every low-paying job, and nobody gave away food—or anything else—for free.

## CALIFORNIA GROWING

After the depression, California continued to grow in population and influence. During World War II, its military installations were

# A DUST BOWL POEM

Many of the dust bowl immigrants stayed in California and built a life for themselves, but they did not forget those desperate days. In 1940, Flora Robertson looked back on them in a sad little poem:

*California, here I come, too*
*With a coffee pot and skillet*
*And I'm coming to you.*
*Nothing's left in Oklahoma,*
*And if apples, nuts and oranges,*
*And if Santy Claus is real,*
*Come on to California,*
*Eat and eat till you're full.*

the staging area for American forces in the Pacific. In the sixties, its college campuses produced a generation of young activists who protested the war in Vietnam, marched for civil rights, and formed a free speech movement that spread to colleges all over the country.

California society has been shaped by many different kinds of people: Native Americans, Spanish grandees, American gold hunters, railroad tycoons, and movie moguls. Each group has left its imprint on the rich history of the state.

# 3 WORKING TOGETHER

*The Capitol in Sacramento*

**V**ariety has always been one of California's strong points. The economy does not depend upon any one industry, nor does the political structure depend upon any one agency or division of government. This diversity makes California unusually quick to spring back in the face of adversity.

## INSIDE GOVERNMENT

California's government is divided into three branches: executive, legislative, and judicial. Voters themselves form a kind of "fourth branch." Three direct participation laws, called initiative, referendum, and recall, give ordinary citizens a chance to shape their own government.

**Executive.** The governor is chief executive officer of the state, elected for a four-year term. No governor may serve more than two consecutive terms, for a total of eight years. The governor appoints state, county, and municipal judges, as well as members of various agencies and commissions. He or she prepares the state budget and submits it to the legislature. He can also veto (reject) measures that the legislature has approved.

California has had some interesting and influential governors over the years. Earl Warren served for ten years, before term limits

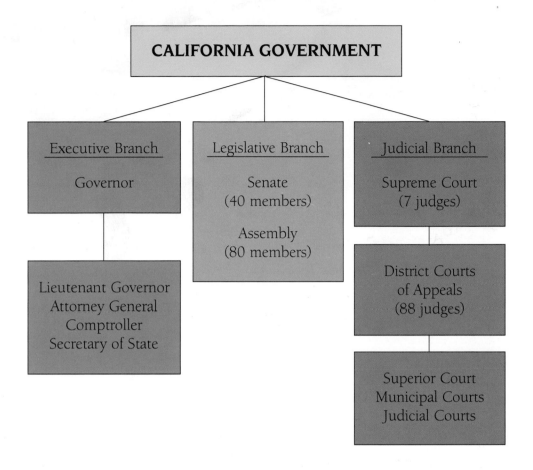

**CALIFORNIA GOVERNMENT**

Executive Branch

Governor

Lieutenant Governor
Attorney General
Comptroller
Secretary of State

Legislative Branch

Senate
(40 members)

Assembly
(80 members)

Judicial Branch

Supreme Court
(7 judges)

District Courts
of Appeals
(88 judges)

Superior Court
Municipal Courts
Judicial Courts

were established, and went on to become chief justice of the U.S. Supreme Court. Ronald Reagan served eight years. The national attention he gained in the office played an important part in his eventual rise to the presidency.

One California family has had a remarkable impact on the California governorship. Edmund G. "Pat" Brown served from 1959 to 1967. His son, Edmund G. "Jerry" Brown, Jr., was also a two-term governor, from 1975 to 1983. Pat's daughter, Kathleen, ran unsuccessfully for the office in 1994.

All the Browns have been liberal Democrats, concerned about social programs and equal rights. The senior Brown improved

*Former Governor Pat Brown talks with residents of the Watts section of Los Angeles and a National Guardsman in an effort to end days of racial riots in 1965.*

welfare programs for California's poor and established a master plan for higher education in the state. Jerry Brown created an agency to protect the rights of migrant farmworkers and appointed liberal judges to the bench.

His methods were less orthodox than his father's, though. The younger Brown lived in a modest apartment instead of the governor's mansion, drove a modest car, and generally rejected the pomp and circumstance that usually goes with high office. "Where but in California could you have a movie star [Ronald Reagan] and a guy who lives like a religious hermit as back-to-back governors?" asked a junior college political science teacher.

The executive branch also includes other officers who serve the entire state rather than any particular district. There is a lieutenant governor, who serves if the governor cannot; a secretary of state, who keeps public records and documents; an attorney general, who serves as the state's lawyer; and a treasurer and a comptroller, who manage state finances.

**Legislative.** The legislature is the lawmaking branch of state government. It is made up of two houses: a forty-member senate and an eighty-member assembly. State senators are elected for four-year terms and are limited to two terms. Assembly members, called

*Former Governor Jerry Brown shakes hands with supporters in New York City during his 1992 presidential campaign.*

representatives, are elected for two years with a maximum of three terms. For a proposal to become law, it must receive a majority vote in both houses and be signed by the governor. If the governor uses his veto power, the legislature can override it by a two thirds majority vote of both houses.

For most of its history, California did not have term limits for senators and representatives. Then in 1990, voters approved a term limit law. Assembly Speaker Willie Brown, who had served in the legislature for 27 years, challenged the law in the U.S. Supreme Court. In March 1992, the court ruled that the term limit law was constitutional. Brown left the legislature, but not public life. In 1995, he was elected mayor of San Francisco, to the delight of his supporters all over the state.

*Willie Brown laughs with President Bill Clinton on the phone during his inauguration as mayor of San Francisco.*

**Judicial.** California has three types of trial courts: superior, municipal, and justice. Each county has one superior court and a number of municipal and justice courts. The superior court hears felonies (major crimes) and civil suits involving over $15,000. Municipal and justice courts hear misdemeanors (minor crimes) and civil matters under $15,000.

When someone challenges the ruling of a trial court, one of five district appeals courts hear the matter. If there is another challenge, the state supreme court is petitioned for a hearing.

**Direct Legislation.** California has a strong tradition of direct citizen participation in the lawmaking process. Through initiative, referendum, and recall, voters can pass new laws, override the legislature, or throw elected officials out of office before their terms expire.

Other states use direct participation measures, but not so widely as California. In the 1990 general election, for example, voters had to decide on twenty-eight different propositions. One of them was the term limit law that unseated Assembly Speaker Willie Brown.

**Local Governments.** A state as big and complex as California must have several levels of government in order to function efficiently. California's fifty-eight counties are governed by five-member supervisory boards, chosen in nonpartisan local elections. A county supervisor is supposed to behave more like a business manager than a politician. This means that he or she should be more interested in sound business practices than political ideology.

California cities are generally run by elected councils and a mayor or professional city manager who sees to the day-to-day

*Police line up in riot gear in case of violence at a Mexican-American Cinco de Mayo celebration in downtown Los Angeles. California has the second largest police force in the country.*

The voters' next target was repeat offenders. Even the most violent of these criminals often served only a small part of each sentence before being paroled back into the community to commit new crimes. It took a particularly vicious crime to bring the situation to a head.

In October 1993, twelve-year-old Polly Klaas was kidnapped from her home and later murdered. The man who confessed to the killing was a two-time parolee with a lifelong criminal record and a history of violence. He was on parole for kidnapping a woman at knifepoint when he walked into the Klaas home and took Polly.

In the next election, outraged Californians passed a tough new sentencing law. "Three strikes and you're out" closed the revolving door for violent offenders. With three convictions, they went to prison for life.

In 1995, another "get tough" measure was proposed to make guilty verdicts easier to obtain. Under current law, California

*A crowd outside the Sonoma County Jail calls for the death penalty for accused mass murderer Ramon Salcido in 1989. There has been a growing demand for capital punishment in the state.*

requires a unanimous vote in criminal cases: All twelve jurors must agree. Fred Goldman, whose son Ron was murdered with Nicole Brown Simpson, led a move to allow a guilty verdict on a 10–2 vote. He argued that "Unanimous verdicts play into [defense lawyers] hands by encouraging them to take strong prosecution cases to trial in hopes of finding one or two unreasonable, biased jurors [who] will delay . . . the system."

**Crackdown on Drunk Driving.** Like every other state, California has its share of crimes that are not committed by career criminals. Driving under the influence is one of these offenses. Every year, police arrest thousands of drunk drivers. Every year, hundreds of others manage not to get caught until they cause an accident.

To cope with the problem, California has one of the strictest drunk driving laws in the nation. A driver is considered to be "under the influence" with a blood alcohol concentration (BAC) of .08 (one or two drinks). First-time offenders face a fine of $350 to $1,000 and up to six months in jail. Two convictions within a seven year period can bring a $1,000 fine and a year in jail.

California doesn't stop with punishing those who break the rules. Many state and private agencies have programs to stop drunk driving before it starts. Community service groups offer free rides home on New Year's Eve and other holidays when drinking is usually part of the celebration. On Saturday nights in many a country town, police drive by the lodge halls at closing time. Just the sight of a squad car makes drinkers think twice about driving home.

A clever way to keep people from mixing alcohol and gasoline is the "designated driver" plan. It has become almost fashionable in trendy California: one person agrees to stay sober and drive every-one else home. To encourage the practice, some restaurants and bars offer a selection of nonalcoholic cocktails for designated drivers.

## EDUCATION AND HUMAN SERVICES

California has a vast network of human services: schools and libraries, parks and recreation, health care, welfare, and child protective services. Many of these programs are mandated, or required, by the state, but operated by the counties.

**Protecting Children.** Child abuse prevention is a good example. By law, a teacher, health care provider, or other caregiver who suspects that a child has been abused must file a report. County social services handle the investigation.

Private groups like Parents Anonymous (PA) work in partner-ship with social service agencies. PA is a national organization with headquarters in California. It deals directly with abusive parents, helping them learn new and better ways to discipline their children.

**Schools.** California's public school system has more than 5 million students and spends $4,608 a year on each of them. A state board of education sets curriculum standards, oversees teacher certification, and administers state and federal funds. Local school districts are responsible for the day-to-day operation of schools in their communities. They hire teachers and other school staff, maintain buildings, purchase books and supplies, and operate bus services.

In the eighties and nineties, California changed the way its

*A young student learns to read.*

schools taught history and social studies. A new multicultural approach acknowledged the contributions of different ethnic and racial groups. Students still learned about the pilgrims who landed at Plymouth Rock, but they also learned about the Native Americans who were there to meet them. They learned about human rights and the dangers of racism.

Though multicultural education has a serious purpose, it also has a lighter side. Some of the study units are as much fun as a role-playing game. At one northern California high school, students studied Native American culture by building an entire village and staging a festival there.

The project affected every class in the school. Native American ideas served as the basis for math, English, reading, history, and social studies projects. Twice a week, the students worked on their village. They built a tule house, a bark lodge, and a small tepee. When the work was done, they threw a party for the whole community, with Native American dancers and Native American foods.

## THE ECONOMY

California's economy is broadly based, with agriculture, aerospace, electronics, entertainment, and manufacturing all contributing to the mix. These industries support thousands of retail and service businesses, from fast-food restaurants and shopping malls to gas stations, supermarkets, and dog groomers. The public sector creates jobs in utilities, highway maintenance, law enforcement, health care, and education.

At the beginning of the 1980s, California had the largest commercial bank in the country, the top six savings and loans, the biggest supermarket chain, and the most TV and movie producers in the world.

By the beginning of the nineties, cracks had appeared in California's economy. Real estate prices soared so high that many families would never be able to buy their own home. A scandal in the savings and loan industry drained millions from the economy. Massive closures of military bases threw thousands of people out

# EARNING A LIVING

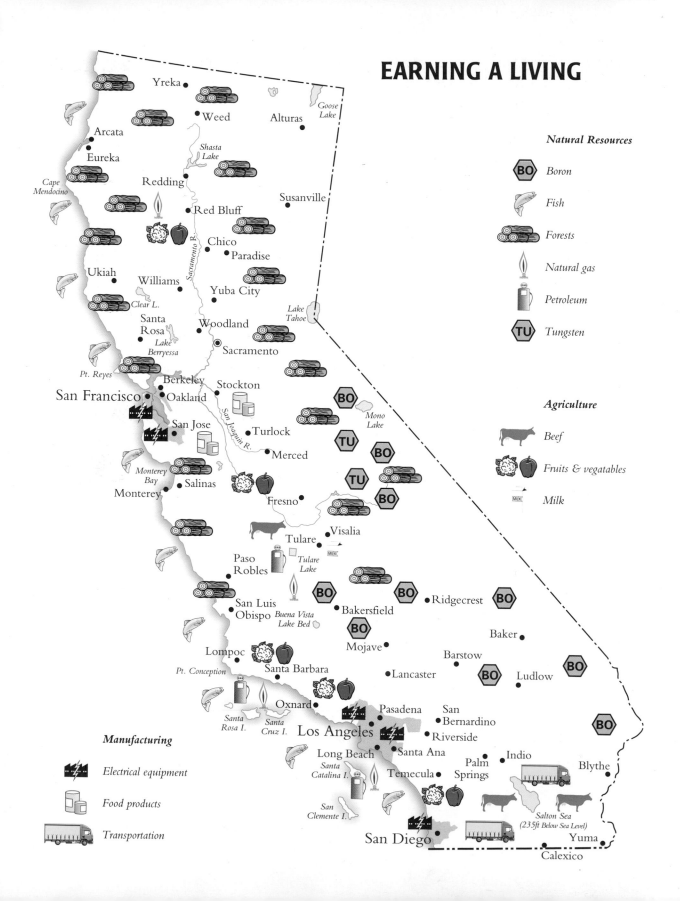

**Natural Resources**

BO — Boron

— Fish

— Forests

— Natural gas

— Petroleum

TU — Tungsten

**Agriculture**

— Beef

— Fruits & vegetables

MILK — Milk

**Manufacturing**

— Electrical equipment

— Food products

— Transportation

Yreka
Weed
Alturas
Goose Lake
Arcata
Eureka
Shasta Lake
Redding
Cape Mendocino
Red Bluff
Susanville
Chico
Paradise
Ukiah
Williams
Yuba City
Clear L.
Lake Tahoe
Santa Rosa
Woodland
Lake Berryessa
Sacramento
Pt. Reyes
Berkeley
Stockton
San Francisco
Oakland
San Joaquin R.
Sacramento R.
San Jose
Turlock
Mono Lake
Merced
Monterey Bay
Salinas
Monterey
Fresno
Tulare
Visalia
Paso Robles
Tulare Lake
San Luis Obispo
Buena Vista Lake Bed
Bakersfield
Ridgecrest
Baker
Mojave
Barstow
Lompoc
Lancaster
Ludlow
Pt. Conception
Santa Barbara
Oxnard
Pasadena
San Bernardino
Santa Rosa I.
Santa Cruz I.
Los Angeles
Riverside
Long Beach
Santa Ana
Palm Springs
Indio
Blythe
Santa Catalina I.
Temecula
San Clemente I.
Salton Sea (235ft Below Sea Level)
San Diego
Yuma
Calexico

*California is number one among the states in the production of lettuce and several other vegetables. It is the nation's leading agricultural state.*

of work. Even "Silicon Valley," the birthplace of the personal computer revolution, slowed its pace of growth.

For the first time in history, large numbers of people began leaving California for greener pastures Between 1991 and 1994, the state lost over a million residents.

Many who stayed faced hardship. Twenty-five-year-old Arturo Garcia works seven days a week at three different jobs, just to stay afloat. Most nights, he gets only four hours sleep. "Sometimes it takes . . . an hour to wake me up. I'm always saying, 'Just five more minutes, just five more minutes.'"

Many experts thought quality of life issues had driven people away. They said that traffic congestion, air pollution, street violence, and earthquakes had finally caught up with Queen Calafia's mythical paradise. A study by economists at the Federal Reserve Bank in San Francisco showed otherwise. People moved away to find jobs, not to escape the California lifestyle.

California-born Brian Austin is typical of those who left. A skilled aircraft mechanic in his mid-twenties, Austin could not find a job anywhere in the state. He ended up taking an entry-level position with a firm in Texas. "They came to California to recruit people

# 1992 GROSS STATE PRODUCT: $788 BILLION

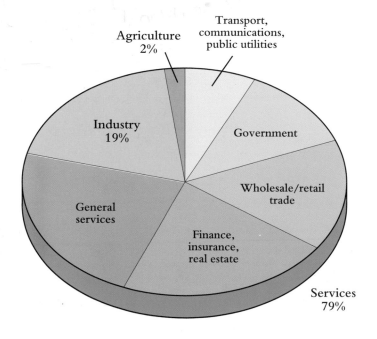

*Homeless people sleep on Venice Beach.*

like me," he said. "They offered a good salary and a bonus . . . even paid my moving expenses."

Like many who left during the eighties, Brian Austin didn't mean to leave California permanently. It just worked out that way. "Living expenses were so much less, especially housing," he explained. "Then I met my wife, and I guess we've just settled in. I don't think I'll ever get back to California now, except for visits."

In the mid-nineties, California began getting back some of its old

energy. The economy weathered the savings and loan scandals. Business groups set to work converting military bases to civilian uses. Job prospects brightened. Though many problems remained, people told each other that the worst was over.

Experienced California-watchers say that's the way of things in the Golden State. California politics get messy now and then. The economy has its ups and downs. Somehow everything seems to work itself out, though. Californians have a knack for survival that has held them in good stead since James Marshall found that gold at Sutter's Mill.

*Grape stompers enjoy making wine the old-fashioned way at a winemaking festival.*

# 4 LIVING TOGETHER

**M**uch has been written about the California lifestyle. According to modern legend, everyone in the state is young, blonde, and gorgeous. They live on salads, salsa, and guacamole, wear the latest designer sportswear, and spend their time shopping, surfing, or lying about at the beach. Every second or third person on the street is a movie star or a rock singer.

The real California is not nearly so glamorous—but it is even more interesting. California has many kinds of people who live in many different ways. There is a large Armenian community in Fresno, a Pakistani settlement near Sacramento, and a thriving Sikh temple in Yuba City. Filipinos and other Pacific Islanders live in many communities up and down the coast. The three largest minority groups are Latinos, Asians, and African Americans.

For most of the twentieth century, Caucasians (whites) have been an overwhelming majority in the state. By the year 2000, they may be one minority among many, as the combined number of Latinos, Asians, African Americans, and others becomes greater than the number of Caucasians.

## LATINOS

Mexican Americans and other Latinos make up the largest minority group in California, with nearly 26 percent of the total population. In 1910, they accounted for only 2 percent of the state's 2,377,549 people. That percentage began to grow during the Mexican revolution. Between 1910 and 1915 thousands came north to escape the war and find work in California agriculture. They lived in barrios, Spanish for neighborhoods, and worked in the fields.

Over the years, Mexican immigrants mixed their traditions with American ones to create a new Mexican-American culture. They had their own way of dressing and speaking, their own fads and cultural values. Most were fully bilingual in Spanish and English. The neighborhood and the family played important roles in the lives of Mexican Americans. They called one another "homeboys"

*A group of Latino children pose for the camera.*

# THE SWALLOW AND THE SONGBIRD

Many California stories have a Spanish or Mexican flavor about them. They have color and fire and romance—and sometimes sadness. This tale is ageless:

The swallows came back as always that year. The sky over Capistrano was alive with them. A songbird, watching them arrive, chanced to notice a pretty young swallow. When she looked his way, he began to sing a fine, soaring melody that touched the swallow's heart.

And just like that, the two were in love.

All summer, they were together. The songbird helped the little swallow build her nest in the eaves of the little church. Sometimes they rested there in the shadows. Sometimes they flew for the simple joy of flying; and sometimes, they sat in the mesquite tree beside the mission wall.

Then came the time that both had dreaded; the time when the leaves begin to turn and autumn nips the air. "Soon I must go," said the swallow, but the songbird begged her to stay.

and "homegirls" and made their own island of belonging in the midst of a hostile society.

In the 1960s, they began moving beyond that island. This was a time of protests and demonstrations for many causes: equal rights for minorities, peace in Southeast Asia, free speech on college campuses. Mexican Americans joined the struggle. People like Ruben Salazar and Cesar Chavez led the fight.

Salazar was a talented writer whose pieces in the *Los Angeles Times* told the hard truth about life in the barrio. He was killed in August 1970, when a protest march exploded into violence.

"The flight is long and dangerous," he said. "So many perish on the journey. Stay here with me. I'll take care of you."

"If I stay here," replied the swallow, "I will surely die. I can't live in this place through the winter."

"Maybe I could go with you," the songird suggested, but the swallow shook her head.

"Then you would be the one to die. You can't fly so far."

The two birds talked for a long time. Finally, they decided that the only sensible thing was for the swallow to go and the songbird to stay behind.

And so they said goodbye, vowing to meet again in the spring. The songbird waited. When the swallows returned to Capistrano, he watched the skies for his beloved. He went to the little church where she had built her nest, and he went to the mesquite tree where they had spent so many pleasant afternoons. He waited there until nightfall. He waited by starlight and by sunlight; he waited in the eaves of the church and the branches of the mesquite tree. He waited and he waited; every spring he waited. Until one day, the swallows returned and the mesquite tree was empty. The songbird waited no more.

Chavez was a migrant farmworker with an eighth-grade education and a dream. Migrants picked crops up and down the state, living in grim labor camps and working for starvation wages. Chavez organized them into a labor union. With strikes and rallies and boycotts, the United Farm Workers of America (UFW) won better wages and working conditions for its members.

## ASIANS AND PACIFIC ISLANDERS

Asians and Pacific Islanders (Filipinos, Samoans, and others

*For over thirty years, labor leader Cesar Chavez strived to improve working conditions for Mexican-American farm workers. Here, he calls for a boycott of Eastern Airlines in a 1989 rally at Washington's National Airport. He advocated nonviolence as the way to achieve justice and equality for all workers.*

from the South Pacific) are the next largest group, with almost 10 percent of the population. Of all Asian groups, the Chinese and Japanese have been in California the longest. The Chinese came during the gold rush and stayed to build the transcontinental railroad. When the Big Four needed workers to lay track, Charles Crocker decided to hire Chinese immigrants. The first all-Chinese crew of fifty men went to work in 1865. By the time the railroad was finished in 1869, ten thousand Chinese workers had helped to build it.

After finishing the job, the Chinese turned to fields such as agriculture, mining, and manufacturing. They lived in their own neighborhoods, establishing large Chinatowns in San Francisco, Los Angeles, and other cities.

Many modern Chinese Americans have moved into the general population but still keep their links to traditional culture. Each September, for example, hundreds gather in San Francisco's Chinatown for the Moon Festival. People dress in lavish ceremonial costumes, and the streets come alive with music and laughter. There are craft exhibitions, kung-fu demonstrations, and plenty of moon cakes to eat. The highlight of the two-day event is a traditional lion dance.

Like the Chinese, Japanese Americans in California have kept their culture alive. Traditional Japanese culture has a way of turning ordinary activities into art forms: Gardeners create wondrous landscapes from plants, stones, and sculptured wood; calligraphers make penmanship beautiful; cooks turn chopping vegetables into a

*A young Asian boy engrossed in his Chinese calligraphy— the art of beautiful writing.*

*Japanese-American girls are wearing colorful kimonos and holding umbrellas and fans.*

performance; even arranging flowers or serving tea is done with full attention to the task of the moment.

As a Zen Buddhist saying goes, "If you walk, just walk. If you sit, just sit; but whatever you do, don't wobble." This love of the commonplace has made Japanese arts popular with Californians of other backgrounds. Community centers and colleges all over the state teach everything from calligraphy to flower arranging.

Prominent Japanese Americans associated with California include actor George Takei of *Star Trek* fame, figure skater Kristy Yamaguchi, and orchestra leader Seiji Ozawa.

## AFRICAN AMERICANS

At the beginning of the gold rush, there were only about one thousand African Americans in California. Some were brought west as slaves, some came as free people, and some came as fugitives from a system that counted them as property. When California became a state, it outlawed slavery but kept many racist laws. African Americans could not vote, testify in court, or own property. Their children could only attend segregated schools.

In spite of these restrictions, some African Americans achieved distinction. During the first half of the nineteenth century, frontiersman James Beckwourth ranged from the Rocky Mountains of Colorado to the Sierras of California. He lived among the Crow and other Native American tribes. They accepted him readily because he was a man of his word—and because he knew as well as they how difficult it was to live in a racist society. In 1850, Jim Beckwourth discovered the Sierra Nevada pass that bears his name.

## JUNETEENTH JUBILEE

Slaves in Texas finally got the word in June 1865: President Abraham Lincoln had set them free! The news was over two years old by the time it reached Texas, but that didn't matter. The former slaves rejoiced, and from that day on, they marked "Juneteenth" as a festival of freedom. Over the years, the custom has spread to California.

Juneteenth brings hundreds of people to Sacramento's McClatchy Park. There's music everywhere and people singing about togetherness, friendship, and freedom. Some bring guitars or harmonicas or old violins to play. The tangy smell of barbecued spare ribs wafts through the air.

"It's a time when we can build tradition," said teacher Patricia Adelekan. "It's an awakening of something that's been hidden for a long time."

Not everyone knows about Juneteenth yet, but each year the Sacramento festival grows bigger and more colorful. It has become a true California holiday because it gives people a chance to celebrate freedom—and have some fun in the bargain.

Allen Allensworth was born a slave in Kentucky. In California, he founded a town where African Americans could live and work and govern themselves. Allensworth, California, prospered for a decade but finally fell victim to the fate of many desert communities: lack of a dependable source of water. In 1971, the Department of Parks and Recreation restored his pioneering settlement as a historic park.

During World War II, African Americans flocked to California to

*Colonel Allen Allensworth, who was born a slave, moved to California and founded a town.*

work in shipyards, steel mills, and aircraft plants. By 1990, more than 2 million African Americans lived in the state.

Partly because of the prejudice they still face, African Americans in California tend to gather in certain areas. The Watts neighborhood in Los Angeles and Hunter's Point in San Francisco have large African-American populations. So do the Bay Area cities of Richmond and Oakland. These urban residents tend to be poor and underemployed.

"It's a place you want out of," said one young woman who grew up in Oakland. Lisa became a hairdresser and moved to a small town that is a three-hour drive from the old neighborhood. She has her own shop, where her clientele includes many Caucasians and Latinos as well as African Americans.

# ETHNIC CALIFORNIA

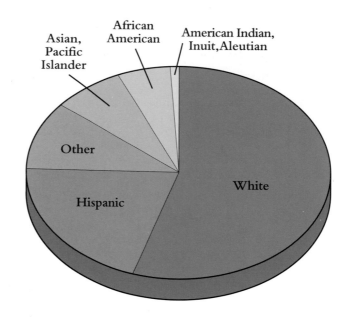

## THE NEWEST CALIFORNIANS

In the 1980s and 1990s, immigrants and refugees from many cultures poured into California: 207,326 entered legally in 1994, with an estimated 105,000 coming illegally. These new arrivals included refugees from the former Soviet Union, Latinos from troubled countries like Colombia and Guatemala, and Southeast Asians from Vietnam, Laos, and Cambodia.

California doctors are seeing tuberculosis from Asia, radiation poisoning from a nuclear power plant failure in the Ukrainian town of Chernobyl, and the signs of neglect and mistreatment from places all over the world. California teachers are trying to educate immigrant children in classrooms where the students speak six or seven different languages. An army of welfare workers, counselors, clergy, job placement specialists, and community volunteers help new Californians of many cultures adjust to their surroundings.

The process is expensive. Most Californians accept that expense for humanitarian reasons. Some resent it, especially when costly services go to people who are in the state illegally. In the 1994 election, voters passed a controversial initiative to deal with the problem. Proposition 187 denied public services to illegal aliens and required teachers, health care workers, and others to report suspected illegals to immigration authorities.

The measure sent shockwaves through California society, espe-

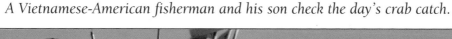

*A Vietnamese-American fisherman and his son check the day's crab catch.*

cially Latino communities. More illegal aliens come from Mexico and Central or South America than from other parts of the world. The border is close and not too difficult to pass over, so thousands cross it every year.

Mexican Americans considered Proposition 187 a slap at all Latinos. They fear a day when a person could get reported simply for "looking Mexican" or speaking Spanish. They also resent the claim that illegal aliens come to California so they can get welfare payments. Actually, most come to work on the state's large commercial farms.

"The Proposition 187 ads showed Mexicans running over the

border, but they never showed us working in the fields," a sixteen-year-old high school student told the *Sacramento Bee*. "My family feels so discriminated against and angry."

This student's family was not alone. Opponents of Proposition 187 moved to block it in the courts. U.S. District Court Judge Mariana R. Pfaelzer ruled that California could not withhold education, health care, or welfare benefits from undocumented immigrants, and it could not require teachers and social service workers to report people to the authorities.

*In San Francisco, hundreds of mostly Latino students protest the passage of Proposition 187 in 1994, which approved a sweeping crackdown on illegal immigrants, denying them access to many public services.*

# RECIPE

## Bean and Cheese Burritos

Most people think that burritos are a Mexican food; actually, they are a Mexican-style California food. They are also delicious and easy to make:

Ingredients:

    2 16 oz. cans Mexican-style refried beans
    6 flour tortillas
    1½ cups shredded cheddar cheese
    about 1 cup finely chopped onions

What to do:

1. Heat the beans: (Ask an adult to help you do this on the stove, in a microwave, or in a small Crock-Pot.)
2. Steam the tortillas just enough to make them warm and flexible. The microwave does this nicely. Stack the tortillas on a plate with wax paper (NOT aluminum foil or plastic wrap) between them. Cover with a moist kitchen towel and microwave for about 3/4 min.
3. Put about ½ cup of beans in a line down the center of each tortilla, leaving about an inch at top and bottom. Sprinkle with chopped onions (about 2 tablespoons) and shredded cheese (about ¼ cup).
4. Fold the top and bottom of the tortilla over the filling, then fold the sides. Your burritos are ready to eat!

## A MULTICULTURAL LIFESTYLE

Alongside the problems that set racial or ethnic groups against one another, there are signs of greater tolerance and understanding. High schools in different parts of the state have multicultural clubs, where students from different cultural, racial, and religious backgrounds come together to share their traditions. Most of these clubs leave studying for the classroom; their purpose is to share experiences. They sample each other's foods, sing each other's songs, celebrate each other's holidays.

# TEN LARGEST CITIES

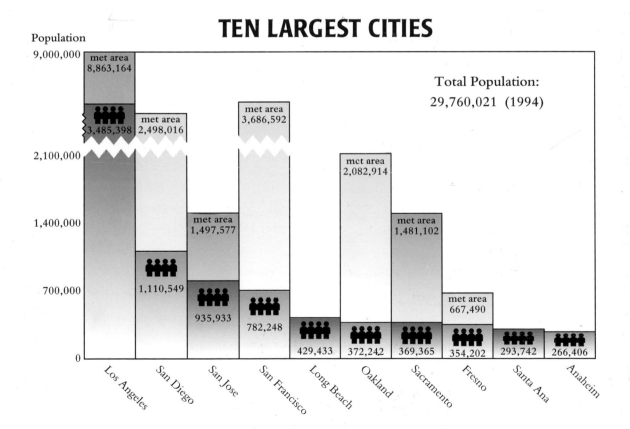

*The many different ethnic backgrounds of Californians are represented in this class photo.*

In many California cities, whole neighborhoods are taking on a multicultural flavor. On Stockton Boulevard in Sacramento, journalist Stephen Magagnini saw a Romanian woman buying a cake from a Chinese bakery, which rents space in a furniture store owned by a Korean and managed by a Latina.

In spite of hopeful signs, California still has its troubles. Different racial and ethnic groups don't always get along. There are people who long for the days when Caucasians were a clear majority and everybody else was supposed to learn *their* way of doing things. There are people who worry that sharing other cultures will mean losing their own.

As the twentieth century draws to a close, California stands halfway between the old way and the new. The challenge of the next century will be learning to live together peacefully and to respect one another's ways. People of goodwill are determined to meet that challenge and to create a way of life that has room enough for all.

# 5 MOVERS AND SHAKERS

California has always produced its fair share of people who break new ground and try new things. Many of these "movers and shakers" have gained national and worldwide fame:

## THE PRESIDENT FROM HOLLYWOOD

In 1981, Ronald Reagan became president of the United States. When he took the oath of office, it was the end of one long journey and the beginning of another.

The first journey began in 1911. Ronald Wilson Reagan was born on February 6 in Tampico, Illinois, the son of an Irish-American shoe salesman. After graduating from Eureka College in 1932, he worked as a radio sportscaster.

Even as an unseen voice on the radio, Reagan had an undeniable charm. In 1937, that charm led to a contract with Warner Brothers Studios in Hollywood. For fifteen years, Reagan's good looks and jaunty grin appeared on movie screens all over the world. In the 1950s, he became interested in politics.

A liberal Democrat in his college days, he became increasingly conservative during his years in Hollywood. His first elective office was the presidency of the Screen Actors Guild. In 1966, he decided to run for governor of California. At the time, that was a bold

*Former President Ronald Reagan greets a crowd at the opening of the Ronald Reagan Presidential Library in Simi Valley in 1991. Behind Reagan are his wife, Nancy, and daughter, Maureen.*

move; a movie star in the statehouse? To many Californians, it seemed unthinkable.

To Ronald Reagan, it made perfect sense. He had ideas, and acting had taught him how to present them. He offered the voters a combination of political conservatism and personal charm.

In the mid-sixties, California's problems were growing as fast as its population. Many people thought government spending was out of control; they were ready for a conservative governor to fix things. If he could reassure people in the bargain, so much the better. Reagan could do all that, so he won the governorship in 1966 and again in 1970.

In 1980, the same combination swept him into the White House and saw him reelected in 1984. Though his programs were not always as successful as he would have wished, Ronald Reagan was an enormously popular president. When he retired after his second term, there was no doubt that the 1980s would always be remembered as "the Reagan years."

## JOHN STEINBECK'S CALIFORNIA

California writer John Steinbeck won the Pulitzer Prize for his 1939 novel *The Grapes of Wrath*. It told of the fictional Joad family and their harsh life as migrant laborers in depression-era California. Steinbeck was born February 27, 1902, in the farming town of Salinas, near the Monterey coast. The California he knew was not a place of gold mines and movie stars. It was a place of lettuce fields and sugar beets; of desperately poor migrants and misfits scraping through life as best they could.

In many ways, Steinbeck was as much a misfit as his characters. He had a restless youth. He studied marine biology at Stanford University but never earned a degree. He moved to New York City to become a writer and nearly starved to death trying to get published. Discouraged, he returned to Salinas and rented a

*Writer John Steinbeck. In addition to his many works of fiction, Steinbeck also wrote* Travels with Charley *in 1962, describing the people and places he saw during his own cross-country trip with his pet poodle.*

shabby little cabin. There he wrote his stories, supporting himself with a string of laboring jobs.

In 1929, he published his first book, a historical novel about the pirate Sir Henry Morgan. It was not a big seller, but at least it was a start. The breakthrough book that made John Steinbeck a literary star was the 1935 novel *Tortilla Flat*. Readers fell in love with the cheerfully eccentric inhabitants of this fictional town on the Monterey coast; people who were so busy living they forgot to remember that they were poor.

John Steinbeck's career stretched over five decades and brought him many honors. In 1940, *The Grapes of Wrath* won the Pulitzer Prize for fiction; in 1962, Steinbeck received the Nobel Prize for a lifetime of outstanding contributions to literature.

# THE GRAPES OF WRATH

In his classic American novel, John Steinbeck describes the Joad family's arrival in California:

At night they bored through the hot darkness, and jackrabbits scuttled into the lights and dashed away in long jolting leaps. And the dawn came up behind them when the lights of Mojave were ahead. And the dawn showed high mountains to the west. They filled [the car] with water and oil at Mojave and crawled into the mountains, and the dawn was about them. . . . They drove through the Tehachapi [mountains] in the morning glow, and the sun came up behind them, and then—suddenly they saw the great valley below them. Al jammed on the brake and stopped in the middle of the road. . . . The vineyards, the orchards, the great flat valley, green and beautiful, the trees set in rows, and the farm houses. . . . The distant cities, the little towns in the orchard land, and the morning sun, golden on the valley. A car honked behind them. Al pulled to the side of the road and parked.

"I want ta look at her." The grain fields golden in the morning, and the willow lines, the eucalyptus trees in rows.

Pa sighed. "I never knowed they was anything like her." The peach trees and the walnut groves, and the dark green patches of oranges. And red roofs among the trees, and barns—rich barns. . . . Ruthie and Winfield looked at it, and Ruthie whispered, "It's California."

## GOOD VIBRATIONS: CALIFORNIANS MAKING MUSIC

The California sound in rock music was a product of the wide-open sixties. The state became a center of experimentation and musical growth, with many talented performers to help the process along. From the song about a drag-racing "Little Old Lady from Pasadena" to acid rock, the California sound grew up during a time of rapid social change.

Early in the decade, the Beach Boys introduced America to a teenage wonderland of sun and fun and surfboards. The group began when three brothers, a cousin, and a neighbor got together to form a band. Brian Wilson, the oldest of the brothers, wrote most of the music. Songs like "Good Vibrations," "Surfin' USA," and "California Girls" became nationwide hits.

The Beach Boys eventually sold more than 65 million records worldwide and played to packed houses throughout the country. They belonged to a land of endless summer. Their songs made teenagers in Minnesota and Michigan and Upstate New York feel like they belonged there, too. That was the secret of the Beach Boys' success. As one of the group explained: "We picture the U.S. as one great big California."

The quartet known as the Mamas and the Papas brought a mellow, more wistful sound to California music, with songs like "California Dreamin'" and "Monday, Monday."

As the sixties counterculture took form, the San Francisco Bay Area became its unofficial headquarters. In Berkeley, University students launched a free speech movement and protested America's role in the Vietnam War. In San Francisco, the Haight-Ashbury district became a haven for social dropouts. The hippies,

*The Beach Boys captured the California lifestyle in their music. They sang mostly about surfboards and cars.*

as they were called, longed for a world of peace and love. To find it, they experimented with meditation and "mind-expanding" drugs. Groups like the Grateful Dead, the Jefferson Airplane, and Creedence Clearwater Revival made counterculture music popular all over the country.

## A PERFORMER'S JOURNEY

In 1974, a single mother named Caryn Johnson moved to San Diego from New York City. She worked when she could find a job, but most of the time she was forced to live on welfare. It was a hectic life, but Caryn Johnson found time to pursue her interest in theater. She helped to start the San Diego Repertory Theater Company then moved to San Francisco in the early eighties.

There she joined another repertory theater. Her fellow actors soon learned that she could play almost any part: ugly ducklings or stunning beauties, children or old people, heroes or villains.

Somewhere along the line she picked up an odd nickname:

*Whoopie Goldberg as Celie in* The Color Purple

Whoopi. The name was a joke at first, but somehow it stuck. "So I thought, why not? I'll be Whoopi," she told one interviewer. Taking one new name meant looking for another. "Whoopi Johnson," she decided, just didn't sound right. She dug into her family background looking for something suitable. When she spotted "Goldberg," she knew she'd found the perfect name.

Whoopi Goldberg put together a one-person show, which she did without makeup or costume changes. With the help of producer Mike Nichols, the show called simply *Whoopi Goldberg* became a Broadway hit.

It gave Whoopi a chance to show her range as a performer. Her roles varied from a male panhandler to a twelve-year-old black girl who thinks life would be perfect if only she had long blonde hair. One night, director Steven Spielberg caught the show. He immediately cast Whoopi as the long-suffering Celie in the movie version of *The Color Purple*.

She has been a Hollywood fixture ever since, playing everything from the psychic con artist in *Ghost* (for which she won an Oscar as Best Supporting Actress) to the mysterious and wise Guinan in *Star Trek: The Next Generation*.

## THE APPLE MAN

In the 1970s, computers were huge machines that gobbled up floor space and strained the budgets of even the largest companies. A young man from the northern California community of Los Altos wanted to change all that.

Steve Jobs, the adopted son of Paul and Clara Jobs, was something of a loner. He didn't work well in groups or know how to make small talk. His mind was quick, creative, and restless. At Reed College in Oregon, he experimented with meditation and Eastern philosophy. That took him to India, where he backpacked across the country in search of a guru, a spiritual teacher who could show him the inmost secrets of life.

By 1975, he was helping his friend Steve Wozniak create a revolutionary computer circuit board. Unlike the behemoths in use at the time, Wozniak's board was small, lightweight, and not too expensive to produce. Steve Jobs was certain he could find a market for it.

The partners worked in Jobs's garage, making boards to sell to computer manufacturers. Wozniak built the boards; Jobs tried to sell them. When his very first sales call produced an order for fifty units, he got an idea: why stop with circuit boards? Why not build a whole computer?

With that question, the Apple personal computer was born.

*Steve Jobs, cofounder of Apple Computer, went on to become president of another computer company called NeXT.*

Wozniak engineered the circuitry; Jobs handled design and promotion. He wanted to create a whole new kind of computer: one that was trim, lightweight, and easy to operate. To describe what he meant, he coined the term "user friendly."

When Apple's first personal computer hit the market in 1977, the company kept its cash receipts in a desk drawer. Three years later, it had total sales of $139 million. In the best California tradition, Steve Jobs became a multimillionaire before he turned thirty. He also became one of those rags-to-riches success stories that have always delighted Californians.

## THE BEST WHO EVER PLAYED

In the National Football League player draft of 1985, the San Francisco 49ers chose a young wide receiver out of Mississippi Valley State University. He had set many school records, including most yards gained by a receiver (4,693 over his college career). He was a gangly young man, with a shy grin and a work ethic that could put other players to shame. His name was Jerry Rice.

After eleven seasons in the NFL, Rice had rewritten the record books. He held career marks for total receiving yards with 13,275, most pass receptions with 820, and most touchdown receptions with 139.

As a player, Rice is self-confident without being boastful. He holds himself to a strict standard of performance. Teammates say he's the first on the field at every practice and the last to leave. During the off-season, when many players like to take it easy, Rice maintains a rigorous workout schedule.

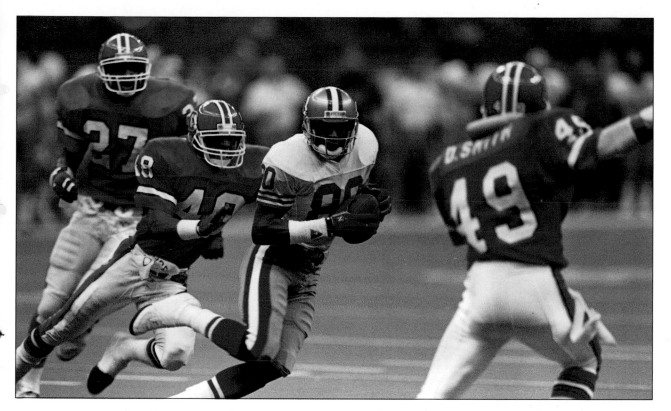

*San Francisco wide receiver Jerry Rice on the run from Denver's Randy Robbins in the 1990 Super Bowl XXIV. The 49ers beat the Broncos, 55 to 10.*

Jerry Rice has become a California institution. Serious fans can recite his statistics and toss in a few stories about his end-zone heroics. Even people who don't like football recognize his name and take pride in knowing that he plays for a California team.

People tend to think of California in terms of movie stars and recording artists. Actually, Californians have achieved distinction in almost every walk of life. From athletes and inventors to presidents and Nobel Prize–winning authors, outstanding citizens have shaped California's reputation as a state that sets the trends for others to follow.

# 6 OUT AND ABOUT IN CALIFORNIA

Touring California is a major undertaking; there is much to see and do in the Golden State. From the mission trail of the Spanish padres, through sprawling cities, quaint gold rush towns, and towering redwood forests, California is a place of many wonders. Let's touch some of the highlights in a quick tour.

## EL CAMINO REAL

We'll begin where the Spanish explorers began in 1769: at San Diego, just across the present Mexican border. It was here that Father Junípero Serra founded San Diego de Alcalá, first of a chain of twenty-one missions that would reach to Sonoma in the northern part of the state. Modern Highway 101 follows a nearly identical route.

The missions were spaced a day's journey apart, and each controlled vast areas of surrounding land. Mission Santa Barbara, for example, had 122,000 acres. The missions themselves were laid out in the Spanish manner, with buildings surrounding a large central courtyard. In addition to a chapel, there were workshops, living and dining quarters, a library, and an infirmary.

Buildings were made of adobe (sun-baked bricks of mud and straw) covered with whitewashed plaster. Red-tiled roofs made a

*The "Mother of Missions"— Mission San Diego de Alcala. The statue of its founder, Father Junípero Serra, was carved in his homeland, the Spanish island of Majorca.*

striking contrast. Most of the missions have been restored, at least in part. Some still function as churches. Mission San Buenaventura is home to an active parish. Its midnight mass on Christmas Eve draws Catholics and non-Catholics alike to the sanctuary.

## SAN DIEGO AND THE SOUTH COUNTIES

San Diego is a city of contrasts. It is a metropolitan center, with high-rise buildings and crowded freeways. It is also a fun-loving beach town, with yacht harbors, quaint seafood restaurants, and mile after mile of glorious beaches.

The San Diego Zoo occupies 125 acres at Balboa Park. The animals live in display areas that resemble their natural habitat. There are no cages here. Instead, there is desert, tundra, grassland, and tropical rain forest. There is also a zoo nursery, where motherless animals are raised by human caretakers.

Downtown San Diego features the beautifully restored Gaslamp Quarter, which is often called "the New Orleans of the West." This

*The Children's Petting Zoo in San Diego*

twenty-one-block area is more than a tourist attraction; it is like a living history museum. It has authentic buildings, fixtures, and furnishings, and an atmosphere of days gone by. There are shops, art galleries, and sidewalk cafes.

## THE DESERT

Less than one hundred miles from the ocean breezes and salt air of San Diego, Palm Springs is the glamour capital of the southern desert. Celebrities like Frank Sinatra, Bob Hope, and Elvis Presley have vacationed here, along with at least five presidents—Eisenhower, Kennedy, Johnson, Nixon, and Ford. An aerial tramway runs from town to the Mount San Jacinto wilderness. The tram is the world's largest and longest, two and a half miles from station to station, with cars that hold up to eighty passengers.

Joshua Tree National Monument preserves a strange and fascinating plant. The Joshua tree is actually a giant cactus, which can grow up to fifty feet tall and live for several hundred years. A young Joshua tree begins its life as a fleshy stalk, thrusting upward from the ground. Limbs form as it grows, and the whole plant bends and twists itself into strange shapes. At sundown, the sight of Joshua trees silhouetted against an orange desert sky is eerie and strangely beautiful.

Farther north in the Mojave Desert, we find towns with interesting names like Twentynine Palms and Apple Valley. Once sparsely populated, these desert areas have become popular resorts. In the 1980s, towns like Victorville and Hesperia grew rapidly as people moved to the desert for affordable housing and cleaner air.

*Silhouettes of Joshua trees against a purple sky and crescent moon. The unusual looking trees were said to have been given their name by early Mormon settlers. The trees' upraised limbs and bearded appearance reminded them of the prophet Joshua leading them to the Promised Land.*

## A PLACE THAT NEVER WAS

Author Helen Hunt Jackson set her 1884 novel *Ramona* in the deserts of Riverside County, near the little town of Hemet. She wrote the book to protest United States mistreatment of Native Americans, but nobody noticed the social commentary. Readers got caught up in the story of Ramona Ortegna, adopted daughter of a Spanish grandee. Her forbidden love for the Indian Alesandro ended in tragedy.

The book was so popular that people began coming to see the place where Ramona and Alesandro were married, the place where he was killed, and the place where she prepared to flee to Mexico with their child in her arms.

Nobody seemed to care that Ramona was a fictional character. Her myth inspired three movies, one sentimental song, and an annual outdoor pageant. Each year, the citizens of Hemet stage the story, with appropriate costumes and pageantry. Each year, people come from long distances to see it and maybe shed a tear for California's very own star-crossed lovers.

West of the deserts, in the Orange County city of Anaheim, lies what is perhaps California's most famous attraction: Disneyland. The park was born in the imagination of Walt Disney and has drawn millions of visitors since its opening in 1955. From the soda shoppes and gift emporiums of "Main Street, U.S.A." to a frontier town of the Old West and a space ship bound for strange planets, Disneyland offers visitors a chance to live their fantasies.

## THE LOS ANGELES AREA

Los Angeles is a sprawling city that fans out into suburbs. Among its many points of interest are fabled places like Hollywood, Beverly Hills, and Westwood. Westwood is a college town, home to UCLA (University of California at Los Angeles). Its broad streets are lined with cafes, coffee houses, and book stores that cater to the student population.

Beverly Hills is known for movie-star mansions and the pricey shopping along Rodeo Drive. Both have been featured in countless movies and television shows. Hollywood itself is no longer the movie capital of California; most of the studios have moved into outlying areas. Television and recording companies still have offices there, and stars still immortalize their footprints in the concrete slabs outside Mann's Chinese Theater.

Griffith Park is the largest city park in California, with 3,761 acres. In addition to riding trails and picnic areas, it includes a 4,000-seat Greek theater, a planetarium, and an observatory. The Griffith Park Zoo houses animals from all over the world in comfortable, naturalistic settings.

Los Angeles has many fine cultural facilities, including the center for the performing arts that contains a symphony hall, a large auditorium, and a small theater for experimental drama. The Los Angeles County Museum of Art is the largest art museum west of the Mississippi River, with more than 250,000 objects in its permanent collection.

One of the best-known sites in the area is the Hollywood Bowl. This natural amphitheater has a stage backed by a shell. The

Hollywood Bowl is famous for its summer program "Symphonies under the Stars."

## THE CENTRAL COAST AND THE BAY AREA

Moving up the coast, we pass through a four-county area of beautiful beaches and pleasant seaside towns. Above San Luis Obispo, we come to one of California's most famous landmarks: Hearst Castle. Built by multimillionaire William Randolph Hearst, the castle is now a state monument.

*Welcome to Hollywood.*

The house and grounds cover 123 acres, including elaborate pools, gardens, terraces, and guest houses. There's even a private zoo. The main house contains some of the world's great art treasures, along with priceless antiquities. There are ceilings from medieval monasteries, fireplaces from Gothic castles, statues from Egyptian temples, and tapestries from Byzantine churches.

San Francisco is a world-class city with landmarks and legends enough for anyone. It marches over the hills between the Pacific Ocean and San Francisco Bay. The famous Golden Gate Bridge

*An aerial view of the Golden Gate Bridge looking north to Marin County. The bridge, opened in 1936, is considered an artistic and engineering wonder.*

*Rows of Victorian houses stand in contrast to the modern backdrop of San Francisco's skyline. The triangular shaped building to the left is the TransAmerican Pyramid, the city's tallest building.*

spans the entrance to the bay, connecting San Francisco to Marin County. The bridge is 4,200 feet long, with towers standing 746 feet high.

The skyline of "The City," as San Franciscans call their home, is one of the most beautiful—and recognizable—in the world. It has appeared in so many movies and television shows that millions recognize its steep hills and Victorian row houses on sight.

Across the bay from San Francisco, Oakland and Berkeley are major cities in their own right. Berkeley is home to a University of California (UC) campus, as well as a number of smaller, private colleges. One section near the UC campus has so many seminaries that the locals call it "holy hill." Oakland is the western end of the transcontinental railway, as well as a major port and shipbuilding center.

## WINE COUNTRY

The center of California's wine country is Napa Valley, where the weather and the soil are perfect for vineyards. Picturesque wineries dot the landscape, many of them made of stone and covered with ivy. In the town of Calistoga, hot mineral springs draw people to fashionable spas.

The wine country also includes Sonoma, Mendocino, and Lake Counties, all of which have vineyards and wineries of their own. Sonoma County is the site of the Luther Burbank Center, a performing arts facility in the city of Santa Rosa. The center was named for the Sonoma County naturalist whose studies of plant genetics led to the creation of several dozen new species. Mendocino County is noted for its redwood trees and seaports that look like New England fishing villages.

Lake County produces wine, but its real claim to fame is Clear Lake, which is about 3 million years old. Some people say that the ancient lake is showing its age. Annual algae blooms give the lake water a greenish cast and give off a strong odor. This annoys boaters and fishermen but does little actual damage. Because the bloom

*A grape picker in the wine country of Napa Valley. Inspired by a visit to the valley, writer Robert Louis Stevensen called its wine "bottled poetry."*

rises from the deep bottom, the lake literally seems to turn inside out. Local citizens have dubbed algae season, "As the Lake Turns," a play on the title of a popular daytime TV drama, *As the World Turns*.

## GOLD COUNTRY

In the foothills of the Sierra Nevada, a number of quiet, historic towns recall the history of the gold rush. Sonora, Columbia, and

*Bodie State Historical Park in the Sierra Nevada—the ghost town remnants of an 1880 mining boomtown. Once home to ten thousand people, this wood-frame time capsule is now an outdoor museum, complete with houses, taverns, and a church.*

Jamestown cluster in Tuolumne county near the center of the mother lode. This one hundred-mile-long system of interlaced veins is made up of gold-bearing quartz.

Back in the days of the forty-niners, Sonora was known as the most violent and lawless town in all the gold country. Prospector William Perkins kept a kind of body count in his journal. He recorded four killings in the third week of June 1850, and six more in the second week of July.

Present-day Sonora is a peaceful, gracious town, beautifully restored to keep its nineteenth-century charm. Victorian houses look as fresh as the day they were built, and the steeple of the wooden church rises over the town's main street. Antique shops, mining-supply stores, and delightful hole-in-the-wall bookstores dot the business district.

In Columbia, twelve square blocks of the old town have been designated a state historic park. Restored buildings include a Wells Fargo office, a Masonic temple, a firehouse, a schoolhouse, and a newspaper office, along with the saloons and stores that once served the miners' daily needs. The main street of the restored area is closed to autos; only horsedrawn vehicles may enter.

Jamestown sits over the exact center of the mother lode. In the early 1990s, it was the scene of great excitement when somebody unearthed a sixty-pound nugget of pure gold. The unexpected discovery had quite a number of people dreaming about a second gold rush. Unfortunately, the dream didn't last for long; the Super Nugget turned out to be an isolated find, not the beginning of a new strike.

## YOSEMITE

Naturalist John Muir was so moved by the Sierra Nevadas that he spoke of them in almost religious terms: "Climb the mountains and get their good tidings. Nature's peace will flow into you as sunshine flows into trees. The winds will blow their freshness into you and

# PLACES TO SEE

Yreka

Weed

Alturas

*Goose Lake*

Arcata

Eureka

*Shasta Lake*

*Cape Mendocino*

Redding

*Lassen Volcanic NP*

Susanville

Red Bluff

*Sacramento R.*

Chico

Paradise

Ukiah

Williams

*Clear L.*

Yuba City

*Lake Tahoe*

Santa Rosa

*Lake Berryessa*

Woodland

**Sacramento**

*Pt. Reyes*

Berkeley

Stockton

*Yosemite*

Oakland

**San Francisco**

San Jose

*San Joaquin R.*

Modesto

Turlock

*Mono Lake*

Merced

*Monterey Bay*

Salinas

Monterey

Fresno

Visalia

Tulare

Porterville

Paso Robles

*Tulare Lake*

San Luis Obispo

*Buena Vista Lake Bed*

Bakersfield

Ridgecrest

*Mojave Desert*

Baker

Santa Maria

Mojave

Barstow

Lompoc

*Pt. Conception*

Santa Barbara

Lancaster

Ludlow

*Santa Barbara Channel*

Oxnard

**Los Angeles**

*Mojave Desert*

**Beverly Hills**

*Santa Rosa I.*

*Santa Cruz I.*

*RODEO DRIVE*

**Griffith Park**

Palm Springs

*Joshua Tree National Monument*

Blythe

**The Los Angeles County Museum of Art**

*Santa Catalina I.*

*Gulf of Santa Catalina*

**San Diego**

*Salton Sea (235ft Below Sea Level)*

**Disneyland**

*San Clemente I.*

**San Diego Zoo**

Yuma

the storms their energies while cares will drop off like autumn leaves."

Of all the magnificent territory in the Sierras, Muir loved Yosemite the most. He was determined to protect this scenic wildland from the builders, speculators, treasure hunters, and settlers who would bend it to their own use.

Thanks largely to his efforts, Yosemite became a national park in 1890. Its 761,236 acres include towering mountains and a valley carved by prehistoric glaciers. The wilderness seems like a place out of time, with crystal waterfalls spilling over jagged cliffs, rock formations taking fantastical shapes, and groves of giant sequoias towering over the land. Some of those sequoias are more than three thousand years old.

The natural splendor of Yosemite makes a fitting end to our California tour. In a sense, we've come full circle, from the forty-niners who risked everything to cross the mighty Sierra Nevada to modern tourists who go there to commune with nature.

In a state known for setting trends and adapting to change, Yosemite is a reminder of other, more permanent values. The mountains, the glacial valley, and the ancient trees are as much a part of the California lifestyle as movie studios and computer companies. John Muir would have loved that.

*THE FLAG: The flag was officially adopted in 1911. It shows a grizzly bear on a green patch and a single red star against a white background and the words "California Republic." A red strip is at the bottom of the flag. It is modelled after the Bear Flag flown by American settlers when they revolted against Mexico in 1846.*

*THE SEAL: Adopted in 1849, the seal shows a grizzly bear representing California. Minerva, Roman goddess of wisdom, stands next to it. A sheaf of wheat and grape clusters stand for agriculture, and a miner with a pick symbolizes the state's rich mineral resources and mining history. In the background, ships represent commerce; the mountains are the Sierra Nevadas. The state motto appears at the top of the seal.*

# STATE SURVEY

**Statehood:** September 9, 1850

**Origin of Name:** Named by Spanish explorers who sailed along the coast in the 1500s, the origin of the name is not clear. *Las Sergas de Esplandia,* a popular Spanish tale published in the early 1500s, told of a fabulous island ruled by a queen named Caliphia. Another possibility is that the name was derived from the Spanish words *caliente fornalla* ("hot furnace)."

**Nickname:** The Golden State

**Capital:** Sacramento

**Motto:** Eureka (from Greek *heureka,* meaning "I have found it")

**Bird:** California valley quail

**Animal:** California grizzly bear

**Fish:** California golden trout

**Flower:** Golden poppy

**Tree:** California redwood

**Colors:** Blue and gold

**Gem:** Benitoite

**Stone:** Serpentine

*California quail*

# I LOVE YOU, CALIFORNIA

This song was sung in 1914 aboard the first ship to sail through the Panama Canal on its way to California. It was not adopted as the official state song until 1951.

Music by A. F. Frankenstein

Words by F. B. Silverwood

**Fossil:** Saber-toothed cat

**Insect:** California Dog-face butterfly

**Marine mammal:** California gray whale

**Reptile:** California desert tortoise

## GEOGRAPHY

**Highest Point:** Mount Whitney—14,494 feet

**Lowest Point:** Death Valley, 282 feet below sea level

**Area:** 158,706 square miles

**Greatest Distance North to South:** 646 miles

**Greatest Distance East to West:** 560 miles

**Bordering States:** Oregon to the north, Nevada and Arizona to the east; Mexico lies to the south

**Hottest Recorded Temperature:** 130° F in Death Valley on July 10, 1913

**Coldest Recorded Temperature:** -45° F at Boca, near Truckee, on January 20, 1937

**Average Annual Precipitation:** 22 inches

**Major Rivers:** Sacramento, San Joaquin, Colorado, Klamath, Russian, Stanislaus, Tuolemne, Merced, Trinity, Eel

**Major Lakes:** Tahoe, Salton Sea, Clear, Goose, Eagle, Mono

**Trees:** cedar, fir, hemlock, giant sequoia, ponderosa pine, California redwood, oak, spruce, maple, Monterey pine, Monterey cypress, aspen, eucalyptus, palm

**Wild plants**: lupine, viola, California poppy, cactus, desert poppies, Joshua tree, burroweed, creosote bush, indigo bush, desert evening primrose, sand verbena, chaparral, beardtongue, fiddleneck, fireweed, Washington lily, myrtle, flowering dogwood

**Animals**: coyote, lizard, rattlesnake, beaver, deer, cougar, fox, mink, muskrat, hare, wildcat, wild burro, bighorn sheep, wolverine, mountain sheep, pronghorn antelope, elk, bear, desert tortoise, horned toad, kangaroo rat, seal, sea lion, otter, dolphin

**Birds**: goose, grouse, mourning dove, quail, turkey, junco, California thrasher, California condor, hermit thrush, mountain bluebird, wood duck, mallard duck, spotted owl, pelican, tern, gull

**Fish**: black bass, striped bass, salmon, trout, abalone, clam, crab, shrimp, lobster, oyster, scallop, perch, tuna, shark, halibut, marlin, sea bass, red snapper

**Endangered Animals**: California condor, Point Arena mountain beaver, gray wolf, black-footed ferret, Pacific pocket mouse, salt marsh harvest mouse, San Joaquin kit fox, Fresno kangaroo rat, giant kangaroo rat, brown pelican, California clapper rail, light-footed clapper rail, yuma clapper rail, San Clemente loggerhead shrike, bald eagle, Eskimo curlew, blunt-nosed leopard lizard, bonytail chub, Lost River sucker, longhorn fairy shrimp, vernal pool fairy shrimp, lotus blue butterfly, mission blue butterfly

*Brown pelican*

**Endangered Plants:** Amargosa niterwort, Bakersfield cactus, beach layia, Ben Lomond wallflower, California jewelflower, California Orcutt grass, Eureka Valley evening primrose, Eureka Valley dune grass, kern mallow, large flowered fiddleneck, Loch Lomond coyote-thistle, marsh sandwort, Monterey gilla, robust spineflower, San Clemente Island broom, San Clemente Island bush-mallow, San Clemente Island larkspur, San Diego button-celery, San Joaquin woolly-threads, slender-horned spineflower, Sonoma sunshine, Tidestrom's lupine, Truckee barberry

## TIMELINE

### California History

**1542** João Rodrigues Cabrilho explores California coast

**1579** Francis Drake lands on coast, claims land for England

**1602** Sebastian Vizcaino surveys Monterey Bay as a site for a Spanish colony

**1769** Spain's first permanent mission established at site of present-day San Diego

**1775** Monterey becomes capital

**1776** Spanish settlers from Mexico reach site of present-day San Francisco

**1810** Mexican rebellion against Spain begins

**1812** Russian fur traders establish Fort Ross north of San Francisco

**1816** Thomas Doak becomes first American settler in California

**1821** Spain grants independence to Mexico

**1822** California becomes part of Mexico

**1826** Jedediah Smith completes first overland trip by an American to California

1831–1836 California revolts against Mexico

1841 First American wagon train arrives in California

1842 John C. Fremont leads U.S. government expedition into California

1846 U.S. settlers in California protest Mexican rule and raise Bear Flag in Bear Flag Revolt

1848 Mexico cedes California and much of the Southwest to United States in Treaty of Guadalupe Hidalgo

1848 Gold discovered at Sutter's Mill

1849 Gold rush begins

1850 California becomes 31st state

1851 Jim Beckwourth discovers Sierra Nevada pass

1854 First transcontinental telegraph line connected

1869 Transcontinental railroad completed, linking California to East Coast

1887 Real estate and population boom in southern California

1890 Yosemite Park established

1906 Earthquake and fire destroy much of San Francisco

1911 First film shot in Hollywood

1930 Dust Bowl refugees from Midwest begin moving to California

1932 Olympic Games held in Los Angeles

1937 Golden Gate Bridge opens

1941 United States enters World War II

1942 Japanese Americans relocated to internment camps

1945 World War II ends; United Nations founded in San Francisco

1955 Disneyland opens in Anaheim

1959–1967 Edmund G. "Pat" Brown, Sr., serves as governor

1962 Cesar Chavez founds National Farm Workers Association (becomes United Farm Workers in 1966)

1964 California becomes nation's most populous state

1966–1974 Ronald Reagan serves as governor

1975–1983 Edmund G. "Jerry" Brown, Jr., serves as governor

1978 State voters approve Proposition 13, a state constitutional amendment cutting property taxes by $7 billion

1984 Olympic Games held in Los Angeles

1989 Earthquake in San Francisco Bay area

1994 Earthquake in Los Angeles

## ECONOMY

**Natural Resources**: petroleum, natural gas, sand, gravel, stone, boron, tungsten, clay, oil, fish, lumber

**Agricultural Products**: milk, beef cattle, greenhouse and nursery products, cotton, almonds, grapes, hay, tomatoes

*Grapes of the Napa Valley*

**Manufacturing:** transportation equipment, electrical equipment, electronic components, computers, military communication equipment, food products, machinery

**Business and Trade:** entertainment, tourism, wholesale and retail trade, finance, insurance, real estate, transportation, communication

## CALENDAR OF CELEBRATIONS

Pasadena is the site of the annual New Year's Day Tournament of Roses. The parade, with its exquisite floral-decorated floats, has been held since 1890. Since 1946, the Rose Bowl college football game has pitted the Pacific Coast Conference champion against the Big Ten champion.

Chinese New Year is celebrated in February during a week of festivities in San Francisco. The grand finale is the Golden Dragon Parade through Chinatown.

Held in February, Snowfest Lake Tahoe is the biggest winter carnival in the West, with skiing, fireworks, parades, and live music.

The Cherry Blossom Festival, held in San Francisco's Japantown in April, features exhibits and a parade.

May Carnaval in San Francisco is a multiethnic parade in May. It includes dancers and samba music, much like Carnaval in Brazil.

*Carnaval in San Francisco*

The Bay to Breakers 7.5-mile foot race in May in San Francisco draws 100,000 runners, walkers, and roller-skaters, many in outrageous costumes.

As part of the Calaveras County Fair, the town of Angels Camp holds its Jumping Frog Jubilee each May. "The Celebrated Jumping Frog of Calaveras County" was Mark Twain's first published success.

Graffiti U.S.A., held in Modesto in the middle of June, celebrates the 1950s (as seen in the movie *American Graffiti*). It features a street fair with 1950s music, arts and crafts, a car show, and a classic car "cruise" downtown.

Celebrate the summer solstice in Santa Barbara with the Summer Solstice Parade with its giant puppets, weird floats and costumes, and a street fair.

The California Rodeo, one of the largest in the nation, has been held in Salinas since 1911. It is held the third weekend of July.

The California State Fair, held in August in the Sacramento area, is a chance to hear top-name singers, watch grape-stomping and pie-eating contests, or view the state's produce and livestock.

The San Francisco Blues Festival is the nation's oldest. It features artists performing outdoors overlooking the bay and the Golden Gate Bridge in September.

Thousands of kilted Scots come to Santa Rosa each September for the Scottish Gathering and Games. Competitions include putting and throwing the stone and caber-tossing. (A caber is a large pole.) There's plenty of bagpipe music and food.

The Doo Dah Parade is a spoof of the annual Rose Bowl Parade held in November in the same city of Pasadena.

The Dickens Fair in San Francisco recreates the Victorian period with costumes, food, and music and dancing in December.

The Christmas season at Yosemite is a great tradition. A three-hour, seven-course medieval-style meal includes food, music, and song. The Lord of Misrule and his pet bear offer amusing antics.

*Ansel Adams*

## STATE STARS

**Ansel Adams** (1902–1984), born in San Francisco, was one of the nation's foremost photographic artists. He was noted for his black and white photos of Yosemite National Park and other wilderness areas.

**Gene Autry** (1907–    ), born in Texas, starred in more than 80 Westerns, wrote more than 250 songs, and starred in a television series. He was known as the "Singing Cowboy." He also owned television and radio stations in California, as well as a share of baseball's California Angels.

**Barbara Boxer** (1940–    ), born in Brooklyn, New York, spent ten years as a California representative to Congress before being elected senator in 1992. She has worked to further the rights of women and reduce military spending.

**Ray Bradbury** (1920–    ), a writer of science fiction novels and short stories, has been a longtime resident of Los Angeles. His many works include *The Martian Chronicles* and *Fahrenheit 451,* about a society in the future that forbids people to own or read books.

**Luther Burbank** (1849–1926), born in Massachusetts, spent most of his life in California. He moved to Santa Rosa in 1875, where he became a leading horticulturist. He developed new species and variants of many fruits, flowers, and vegetables, including the potato, tomato, corn, and peas.

**Edgar Rice Burroughs** (1875–1950), born in Chicago, lived just north of Los Angeles on an estate he named Tarzana, after his famous fictional character Tarzan. A nearby town now bears the name Tarzana. Burroughs wrote a series of novels beginning with *Tarzan of the Apes,* about a boy raised by apes in an African jungle.

*Cecil B. DeMille*

**Cecil B. De Mille** (1881–1959) was a pioneer movie director and producer. His epic films, often dealing with Biblical or historical subjects, include *The Ten Commandments* in 1923 and a remake in 1956.

**Joan Didion** (1934–    ) wrote *Run River,* a novel about her native Sacramento Valley, as well as many other novels, including *Play It as It Lays* and *A Book of Common Prayer.* She has also written essays and film scripts.

**Walt Disney** (1901–1966) was born in Chicago and moved to Hollywood as a young man. In 1928 he created Mickey Mouse. By 1940, he had established his own studio and developed full-length cartoons, including *Fantasia, Pinocchio,* and *Snow White and the Seven Dwarfs.* He also developed Disneyland near Anaheim in Orange County.

**Isadora Duncan** (1878–1927) grew up in San Francisco before becoming an actor and dancer in New York then London and Athens. She was a great influence on modern dance, rebelling against formal classical ballet and using dance as an individual form of expression. She lived abroad most of her career and established dance schools for children in France, Germany, and Russia.

**Dianne Feinstein** (1933–   ) was the first woman to become a senator from California. She was also the first woman to become mayor of San Francisco. Crime prevention, environmental preservation, and education have been key issues for this Democrat.

**Danny Glover** (1948–   ), an actor, was born in Georgia but raised in San Francisco. He has starred in many movies, including *Places in the Heart, The Color Purple,* and the *Lethal Weapon* series.

**Samuel Golden** (1882–1974), a Polish immigrant, was one of the original partners in Metro-Goldwyn-Mayer, founded in 1924. He soon became an independent producer, developing major stars and authors.

*Danny Glover*

**William Randolph Hearst** (1863–1951) was the son of California Senator George Hearst and Phoebe Apperson Hearst, a noted philanthropist. William built a communications empire with a chain of newspapers, magazines, and radio stations. The classic movie *Citizen Kane* was based on Hearst's life.

**Billie Jean King** (1943–   ), a tennis star, was born in Long Beach. She held women's singles championships in England, the United States, Australia, Italy, and France. She is also well known for her efforts on behalf of women's tennis.

*Billie Jean King*

**Louis L'Amour** (1908–1988) was known for his 86 works of Western fiction. Born in North Dakota, he was a longtime resident of Los Angeles.

**Dorothea Lange** (1895–1965), a photographer, moved to San Francisco from the East Coast in 1918. Her most notable photos were of migrant workers during the Great Depression and of Japanese people held in U.S. Relocation Centers during World War II.

**Jack London** (1876-1916), born in San Francisco, was the author of *The Call of the Wild, White Fang,* and many other books and stories. He was one of the country's most widely read authors because of the action and adventure in his stories. His writings often explored the struggle for survival of characters with primitive, raw emotions.

**Aimee Semple McPherson** (1890–1944), an evangelist and faith healer, settled in Los Angeles in 1918 and founded the Four Square Gospel Church. She also broadcast her message on the radio. At her death, her church had several hundred branches in the United States and Canada (her native land).

*Marilyn Monroe*

**Marilyn Monroe** (1926–1962), a Los Angeles-born actress, made more than 15 movies during the 1950s, including *The Asphalt Jungle* and *Some Like It Hot.* She became a figure of glamour and style, and her death at the young age of 36 increased the public's fascination with her life. She is one of the most written about stars of the twentieth century.

**Julia Morgan** (1872–1957), the first woman to graduate from the state university in mechanical engineering, went on to become an architect. Her first major work was the rebuilding of the Fairmont Hotel after the

San Francisco earthquake and fire of 1906. Her most famous work, however, was the creation of William Randolph Hearst's estate at San Simeon.

**Richard M. Nixon** (1913–1995), thirty-ninth president of the United States, was born in Yorba Linda. Nixon served as a U.S. representative to Congress and as vice-president during the Eisenhower Administration. Running for president on the Republican ticket in 1960, he was narrowly defeated by John F. Kennedy. He ran again in 1968 and defeated Hubert H. Humphrey to become president. He was re-elected in 1972, but forced to resign over the Watergate scandal in 1974. Nixon was the first United States president to travel to China. His term was also marked by controversy concerning the Vietnam War.

**George S. Patton** (1885–1945), born in San Gabriel, became known as "Old Blood and Guts" because of his daring and ruthlessness as a commander of U.S troops in Europe during World War II. He commanded Allied troops in North Africa and Europe during the war and was the commander of the Third Army, which crossed France and fought in the Battle of the Bulge in 1944. In 1945, he commanded United States occupation forces in Europe.

**Linus Pauling** (1901–1994) won a Nobel Prize in chemistry in 1954 for his discoveries about molecular structure and chemical bonds. He won a Nobel Peace Prize in 1962 for his efforts to win a nuclear test ban. Although born in Oregon, he received his Ph.D from the California Institute of Technology and taught in California universities most of his life.

**Ronald Reagan** (1911–    ) was elected President of the United States in 1980 and served two terms, known as "the Reagan years." With his abilities as a communicator and his personal style, he was a popular president. Although born in Illinois, he traveled to California where he signed on as an actor with Warner Brothers. He also served as governor of California for eight years, elected in 1966 and 1970. During his presidency, he advocated conservative social and economic policies.

**Malvina Reynolds** (1901–1978) was a folk singer and social activist who opposed the Vietnam War. Born in San Francisco and a longtime resident of Berkeley, one of her most famous songs is "Little Boxes," a song about conformity and uniformity, which has been recorded by Joan Baez and others.

**Sally Ride** (1951– ), born in Los Angeles, was the first American woman in space when she flew with a *Challenger* mission in 1983. In 1984, she returned to space aboard the *Challenger*. She was part of the commission that investigated the explosion of the 1986 *Challenger* mission and is the author of *To Space and Back*.

**Charles Schultz** (1922– ), born in Minneapolis, Minnesota, and a longtime resident of California, is well known to fans of Charlie Brown, Lucy, and Snoopy as the cartoonist behind the *Peanuts* comic strip. His comic strips are popular with children and adults.

**Isaac Stern** (1920– ), an outstanding violinist, was born in Russia but emigrated to San Francisco at age one. He made his debut with the San Francisco Symphony when he was eleven. He has played and recorded with major orchestras around the world and has helped the careers of many other important musicians. He also led the successful movement to save New York City's Carnegie Hall from demolition in 1960 and was influential in the creation of the National Endowment for the Arts in 1964.

**Elizabeth Taylor** (1931– ) was born in England but became a state resident and a major Hollywood star as a child. At age 13, she starred in

*National Velvet.* As an adult, she starred in *Cleopatra* and *Who's Afraid of Virginia Woolf.* She is also known for her life of glamour and wealth.

*Elizabeth Taylor*          *Shirley Temple*

Shirley Temple (1928–   ) was a nationally known movie star by the time she was six years old. Born in Santa Monica, she was a talented actress, singer, and dancer. Temple starred in *Little Miss Marker, The Littlest Rebel, Rebecca of Sunnybrook Farm,* and many other movies during the 1930s. She received an honorary Academy Award in 1934. Retired from acting by 1950, she later served as U.S. representative to the General Assembly of the United Nations, U.S. ambassador to Ghana, and Chief of Protocol of the United States.

**Earl Warren** (1891–1974), born in Los Angeles, became Chief Justice of the United States Supreme Court in 1953. He had served three terms as governor of the state. As Chief Justice (1953-1969) of the Supreme Court, he presided over a revolutionary period in the history of the Court. One of the Court's most important decisions during this period was to strike down school segregation as unconstitutional. In 1964, he headed a presidential commission to look into the assassination of President John F. Kennedy.

## TOUR THE STATE

**Lava Beds National Monument** (Modac and Siskiyou counties) This is a 46,560-square acre preserve of chasms and caves formed by prehistoric volcanoes.

**Columbia State Historic Park** (Columbia) Twelve blocks of restored buildings recreate the town during gold rush days. Buildings include a Wells Fargo office, a Masonic Temple, saloons, stores, firehouse, schoolhouse, and newspaper office.

**Yosemite National Park** (Tuolemne, Mariposa, and Madera counties) Visitors come to this national park to see spectacular natural attractions such as Bridalveil Fall, Yosemite Falls, Half Dome, El Capitan, Mirror Lake, and Yosemite Valley.

**Sequoia and Kings Canyon National Parks** Mount Whitney, the state's highest point and the General Sherman giant redwood (275 feet) are

*Wells Fargo Express business office*

located within Sequoia. Kings Canyon, just north of Sequoia, also features great groves of redwoods, including the General Grant (267 feet).

**Death Valley National Park** This is one of the world's hottest and driest places. The area contains the country's lowest spot, Badwater, which is 282 feet below sea level. At its highest point, Telescope Peak, Death Valley is 11,049 feet above sea level. The area features a wealth of geological features: sand dunes, sculpted rocks, canyons, mountains, and volcanic craters.

*Sand dunes of Death Valley*

**Sea World** (San Diego), This marine zoological park features killer whales, dolphins, sea lions, otters, and walruses. It also includes rides, aquariums, marine life exhibits, a marina, and research labs.

**Disneyland** (Anaheim) This is a gigantic theme park near Anaheim. It was created by Walt Disney and features many "lands," including Fantasyland, Frontierland, Adventureland, Tomorrowland, Main Street U.S.A., Critter Country, and Mickey's Toontown.

**Knott's Berry Farm** (Buena Park) Founded as a roadside stand in 1920, today this is a large amusement park. The park is divided into five areas representing different periods in the state's history.

**Universal Studios Hollywood** (Universal City) Take the "Back to the Future" ride here or a backlot tour to see where some of your favorite movies were made. Watch demonstrations of special effects or see a television show or movie being filmed.

**Mission San Juan Capistrano** This is one of the 21 missions founded in California by the Spanish. Visitors tour the mission buildings and stop in the museum rooms dealing with the various periods of the mission's history, including Native American, Spanish, and Mexican.

**Monterey Bay Aquarium** (Monterey) This is one of the largest aquariums in the world, with displays of more than 500 species. It includes a two-story sea otter exhibit and a three-story kelp forest.

**Winchester Mystery House** (San Jose) This house has 160 rooms, 2,000 doors, 13 bathrooms, 10,000 windows, 40 staircases, and many secret passageways. The owner, heiress to the Winchester fortune (rifles and guns), and her servants needed maps to find their way around. The heiress, a widow, began construction after consulting a seer who said that continuous building would appease the spirits of people killed with Winchester guns. Construction went on 7 days a week for 38 years.

**Alcatraz Island** (San Francisco Bay) Take a guided tour of a former maximum security federal prison. Al Capone, Machine Gun Kelly, and Robert Stroud, "The Birdman of Alcatraz," were once jailed here.

**Rim of the World Drive** (San Bernardino County) This scenic drive winds for 40 miles with views of Lake Arrowhead, Big Bear Lake, and other panoramic views.